SURFI...

Steve Pike

book 4

About the author

In a journalism career spanning 17 years, Steve Pike used to work the 'graveyard' shift at newspapers to give him days free to surf. He has written, designed, illustrated and edited at newspapers and magazines in Cape Town, Johannesburg, East London, Hong Kong and Melbourne. In 1999, Pike, who has an Honours degree from Rhodes University, got wise by combining his two passions – words and waves – into a career as an editor, freelance writer and creator of zany surfing portal *Wavescape.co.za*.

About the design team

Zigzag Magazine, which celebrated its 25-year anniversary in 2001, was approached to assist because of its position as one of South Africa's leading authorities on surfing. The Zigzag team, under publisher Craig Sims, are surfers who have grown their magazine into a top product. Designer Jake Oberholzer brought his creative skills from the magazine into play, working between *Zigzag* deadlines, adding life and colour to the content.

First Published in 2001 by Book
PO Box 12378, Mill Street, Cape Town, 8010, South Africa

ISBN 1-919833-15-3

Reproduction by Cape Imaging Bureau
Imaging by Syreline Process
Printed by CTP Book Printers, Parow

CONTENTS

PAGES

ACKNOWLEDGMENTS

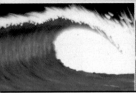  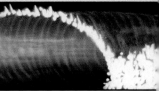

The biggest thanks goes to the surfing community of South Africa, especially those who donated artwork, photographs and stories to Wavescape.co.za, the basis for this book. Their evolving commentary and youthful enthusiasm have been a constant motivating force.

To have such a zoomed–in view of a community in progress is almost better than the view from the Supers carpark at Jeffrey's Bay! When I inadvertently mentioned a semi-secret spot or made mistakes in content, readers reprimanded me firmly but fairly. In a few cases, their rightful indignation gave me a lesson in respect.

A couple of criticisms can be more valuable than a pile of praise, although the many positive comments gave me the confidence and focus to know what I was doing right.

Deep thanks must go to Janet Heard, my long-suffering partner and ex-member of the Camps Bay milkwood crew. Her strong journalistic background, which has gifted her with a no-compromise commitment to quality and ethics, gave me a solid base from which to work. Thanks Jan.

I also appreciate the enthusiasm and impeccable journalistic abilities of Tony Heard, my father-in-law who should still be surfing. Also to Derek Jardine, Tony's old mate, for entrusting me with his precious old photos and complete, untattered collection of *South African Surfer* magazines, which must be a national treasure!

A big thanks to the *Zigzag* crew who worked patiently to deadline with design, and tightened up many areas in the text. Thanks to Craig Sims, Jeremy Saville and Craig Jarvis. Well done Jake for his design, which is just right. Back in Cape Town, to the publishers who worked behind the scenes to pull off a quality product. Thanks to Francois for his good-natured management of the publishing process, and to Ross for the remorseless harassment that made me turn the idea into reality.

To Paul Botha, veteran surf journalist, thanks for the History chapter, and the interesting chats. I appreciate his attention to detail.

Heartfelt thanks to John Whitmore and his wife Shirley for trying to accommodate me on several attempted dashes to Elands Bay. A beanie off to Robin Auld, a roots surfer, musician and one of the country's foremost songwriters and poets. His Foreword sums it up.

Thanks to Callan Emery for photographs, years of advice and encouragement at times when I felt ready to implode with the bubble-bursting Dot Coms. Also for updating the site and surf report when I was away.

All the best in good karma to contributors of text and pictures, including Will Bendix, Byron Loker, Laurence Platt, Mark Muller, Hagen Engler, Alex Urbaniak, Caspar Greeff, Liz Kruger, Peter Deacon, Chip Snaddon, Guy Antoine, Guy Suddes and

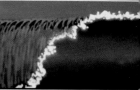

Glenn Hollands, who gave me valuable feedback on the shark chapter.

Many thanks to *Wavescape* photographer Pierre Marqua – your rampant stoke is enough to fell an elephant! Thanks also to Glen Wolter, official *Wavescape* big-wave photographer.

I am indebted to Zaheer Bhyat and Max Kaizen, my original partners in *Wavescape*, who helped me find my feet. I appreciate what you did. In the same vein, thanks to Glen Thompson for his business encouragement and stoke in keeping up the momentum with exciting ideas and plans. Also to Michelle Dorrington and Matt Barker for fun and chaos in the office.

In my research for Wavescape.co.za, I came across Professor Mark Jury's book *Surfing in Southern Africa*, a classic in our surf literature. In the early days Professor Jury kindly allowed me to use descriptions from his book. Since then empty spaces were filled in, or spot descriptions rewritten, by *Wavescape* readers.

Many visitors to the website helped lay the foundations for this book. They made valid suggestions, updated surf spots and sent stories, screensavers, articles or art. My old Cape Town friend Rob Abel gave me many tips and updates. Thanks for fixing my big-wave gun! To Ian Jamieson, who lives at Yellowsands, thanks for the reports and the many tidbits of news and creative bursts from the Eastern Cape. Thanks also to Ian Hunter of the Marine Meterological services in Pretoria for winter storm data.

Several artists added colour and culture to the website and the book. Special thanks to Ruan Benade for the *Wavescape* screensavers and Pete Brandt for helping with the logo. Thanks also to Paul Cumes, Liz Kruger, Rob Hooper, Rowan Thompson, Gary Baker, Tertius Watson and Mark Herbst. Thanks to those whose names I lost or were anonymous!

Thanks to Chris Bertish, our famous big-wave hellman, for his diaries, filled with stoke and energy. Also to Mike Van Der Wolk for advice and help and to *Indies Explorer* skipper Gideon Malherbe for help with the oceanography section and general grammatical issues.

There are many people I should thank (an entire Web community in fact) but then this book would just be filled with names. However, if your name is not in the list, please accept my apologies.

Thanks also to Deon Louw, Peter Lehman, Stan de Jager, Shayne Minott, Etienne Beneke, Shaun Delport, Leigh Forbes-Ewan, Wayne Stewart, Neil Boister, Leslie Koen, Fawzia Collier, Wayne Duncan, Jan Rasmussen, Garth Robinson, Shaun Noon, Tich Paul, Glen Row, Richard Sills, Colin Fitch, Rob Houwing, Cass Collier, Ian Kabot, Leslie Koen, Lian van Rensburg, Philip Desmet, Stu Kelly, Adin Jeenes, Andrew van der Merwe, Baron Stander, Russ Andraos, Pritt from PE and Greg Swart.

PREFACE

To the surfing community of South Africa, this is your book.

This book focuses on three things: our culture, community and coastline. As a cultural reference, it tries to aggregate elements in the collective unconscious of the coastal community. It is also a resource, providing a factual outline of our shores and the weather that brings us waves.

The weather analysis is presented through a surfer's eyes. However, don't use it as a study aid for a meteorology degree – it contains little technical or scientific data. Instead, it is an attempt to empower readers with tools for interpreting South African weather patterns and swell movement.

It may help your quest for the 'grail' you seek – that empty curling tube. There is a string of 'pearls' strung along our coast. This book reviews a good proportion of our world-class surf spots. To find the hidden ones, you must give the password to the gatekeeper. This might mean befriending a local from the area, but only if you have time, and more than a little humility and respect.

The opening chapter deals with surf missions around the SA coast. The shark overview dispels certain myths that unfairly malign this magnificent creature. If you're on a surfari from another clime, you might find the Frequently Asked Questions section helpful.

It has been my aim to lace the facts with a dash of humour and a splash of colour. Throughout the coastal regions, there are anecdotal stories, relevant to that area, by local surfers, which illustrate the richness and variety of our culture and our coastline. A Surfrikan Slang glossary gives a humorous glimpse of South African semantics, with an emphasis on surf-speak.

The origins of the book come from the website Wavescape.co.za, which, as a portal, has been publishing the thoughts, aspirations and anecdotes of South African surfers since 1998. The website was conceptualised in 1996 in Melbourne, Australia. As a night-shift journalist, I would often surf the Web when missing my homeland, despite the occasional good wave at Bells Beach, Winki Pop and Gunnamatta. But I found a lack of quality surf websites on South Africa.

I began researching a way to properly express our home-grown subculture.

The surf travel dream.

A society with 'sosatie' as a word does not have to wear a baseball cap backwards with '*New York Yankees*' on it!

One year later, Wavescape was launched in Cape Town. By early 2001, the site was bulging with information, threatening to engulf its webmaster, who came to be known as Spike from the 'From' field in Wavescape's popular surf report e-mail.

Enthusiastic readers, with great goodwill, contributed to content. This resulted in an almost complete overhaul of the spots section. They flooded the site with graphics, photos and textual contributions until the website grew to more than 1,200 pages, 2,000 images and 22,000 hyperlinks.

With bandwidth on the low side in South Africa, I received e-mails from locals who urged me to write a book. There were also rumours of surfers holed up in Transkei campsites clutching photo-copied versions of the site.

Surfing South Africa celebrates our lifestyle and promotes our country. Even when cultures clash and language is misunderstood, the universal lexicon of the perfect tube brings a common thread to this brotherhood. Now we need to find a way to stop dropping in on each other. — *Steve Pike (Spike)*

HOW TO USE THIS BOOK

Surfing South Africa has been designed as a general guide and resource. The information does not guarantee that you find the more remote surf spots. You won't find detailed maps showing you how to get there. Rather buy a coastal map and use it with the book. There are many place names or landmarks that will give you clues. However, unlike some surf guides overseas, we believe in encouraging a spirit of adventure. Nothing is given to you on a silver platter. Going on a surfari is much more fun if you feel like a pioneer. Besides, most surf spots are in, or near, large towns, which makes them possible to find. To get to rural surf spots, check out your map or bribe the locals. We have left out spots likely to cause a civil war. Also, slang terms are explained in the chapter Surfrikan Slang (p. 164).

FOREWORD

hen Steve asked me to write this foreword it got me wondering about the nature of southern African surfing. Is there a fundamental difference between surfing here and surfing anywhere else? What defines our surfing? Is it the flowing lines of a Natal goofy-foot, carving backside like he's never worn a wetsuit? Is it a Cape hell-man, blind with spray, hauling himself over the ledge on a feathering Kom freefall? Perhaps it is not the surfers, but the places that must count. We have so much to be grateful for. Even with the increased crowd pressure of recent years, the combination of cosmopolitan lifestyle and uncrowded surf availability is hard to match. If you're prepared to look a little further, you can surf with a few mates in absolute desolation and be home in time for a pizza and a movie. And that's if you live in town. Drive for a day and you will have waves for Africa in the most epic locations. We are so blessed with the ocean's abundance, we forget how to count our blessings. We waste time complaining about the crowds, the paddleskiers, the body-boarders, the long-boarders, the short-boarders, the soul guys and the logo guys. I don't care what you ride. A waterman is a waterman. They have manners and a desire to explore.

South African perfection.

Hopefully, this book will encourage the spirit of both. One thing is for sure, there are plenty of waves out there, enough for everyone. And perhaps that's the key to surfing in Africa. We still have space, and we still have time. Time to avoid the ugly stuff so prevalent in more crowded climes. Go and explore, but remember your manners. And if a strange face paddles out, say howzit. It'll make things better, especially when you need a hand getting your car out of the sand.

– Robin Auld, 2001

Dreaming the surfer's dream: J–Bay lines.

An artist's impression of Southbroom, KZN.

The name of the first person on the southern tip of Africa to ride a wave standing up is blurred by time. However, we do know that South Africa's surfing history is a rich tapestry of colourful characters and events that began in the late 1930's and early 1940's when lifesavers on the Durban beachfront began to stand on their heavy 18' wooden boards and ride the breakers.

Originally, surfers were beach sportsmen – lifesavers, divers or spear fishermen. Their boards were copied from Australian designs. After World War II, Durbanite Fred Crocker invented the 'Crocker Ski', a light timber frame covered with canvas and impregnated with aeroplane dope. It had paddles tied to the nose. According to the stories, many of the first waves were

caught on a 'Crocker Ski', with the rider standing, holding and leaning back on the string and digging a paddle to angle right or left to 'catch a broadie' when the waves were 'play'.

The beach culture began to flourish in Durban from about 1947. Ernie Thompson and Brian van Biljon were already the 'older guys' by the time a bunch of local youngsters began hanging out at South Beach at this time. According to Derek Jardine and Anthony Heard, this group included Cliff Honeysett, George Bell, Bruce Giles, Derek and Leith Jardine, Raymond and Anthony Heard, 'Chookie' Salzman, Harry Bold and Shorty Bronkhorst.

Jardine says he rode his first wave in 1948 on a board borrowed from Thompson. In 1951, the South Beach

South Beach, Durban – early 1950s.

crew founded the South Beach Surf-board Club, the first official surfing club in South Africa.

Meanwhile, the first stirrings had occurred in Cape Town. By 1954, perlemoen and crayfish diver, John Whitmore, in his early 20s, built the first foam surfboard from designs he saw in an imported *Findiver* magazine. Carving up a block of newly invented Polystyrene foam, he covered it with muslin soaked in Cascamite glue and sealed it with PVA to stop the coating of polyester resin from eating the foam.

He began building 10', 25 kg surf-boards in his garage, which were used to surf waves around the Cape Penin-sula. A rumour of 'lightweight' boards spread to Durban, and John started

supplying people like Barry Edwards and Baron Stander.

Deliveries to Durban led to Whitmore pioneering surfing in Mossel Bay, Port Elizabeth, East London, Buffalo Bay, Jongensfontein and the beachbreak at Cape St Francis. He also discovered Elands Bay on the West Coast, first ridden in 1957.

The arrival of Epoxy resin – compatible with styrene foam – made glassing easier. Whitmore's fortuitous meeting with Dick Metz, a Californian hitchhiker, greatly influenced our history. Returning home, Metz worked with schoolfriend 'Grubby' Clark, who was moulding surfboard blanks from polyurethane foam. Denser than styrene, they were easier to shape and could be glassed using lighter polyester resin.

In the 1960s the surfing cult took off. Through Metz, Whitmore, now a Volkswagen salesman, imported Clark Foam blanks from California for his now-thriving Whitmore Surfboards business. Metz also put him in contact with John Severson, who sent him *Surfer* magazines sold in South Africa by subscription.

Whitmore owned the first Kombi made in South Africa and invented the first surfboard roof racks. Trips to the VW factory in Port Elizabeth took him past Jeffrey's Bay. His tales of perfect waves led to Capetonians Gerald 'Gus' Gobel and Brian 'Block' McClarty becoming the first humans to paddle out at the Point. Of course, dolphins pioneered the famous waves at Jeffrey's Bay and had already been 'riding' it for thousands of years.

Back in Durban, popout foam boards appeared in 1963. Max Wetteland, George Thomopolous (later Thompson),

Ant van der Heuvel and Robert McWade were the stars. In Cape Town, Whitmore gave up his VW job and started blowing Clark Foam blanks.

Filmmaker Bruce Brown arrived to shoot *The Endless Summer*. Again through Metz, Brown contacted Whitmore. After showing them the Peninsula, he set them up with big game hunter Terence Bullen, who took them to Cape St Francis, where they scored classic two-foot surf they described as 'the most perfect wave in the world'. The film was a hit. Soon, every surfer wanted to visit South Africa.

In 1964, Wetteland, Stander and Harry Bold built the first Safari surfboards in Durban. SA's champion was invited to the first World Surfing Championships at Manly Beach in Australia. No contest had ever been held in SA. Deciding a champion was difficult, so the three drew straws, and Wetteland became the first South African to compete overseas. Midget Farrelly won the event.

Whitmore brought out Brown's movie *Waterlogged*. After selling up to nine shows a day for nine weeks at the Labia Theatre, Cape Town, he took it to Port Elizabeth and East London. Harry Bold put it on in Durban. After Hollywood's *Gidget* movies and the first Beach Boys album – depicting a surfer riding Hawaii's Sunset Beach – everybody wanted to surf.

The SA Surfriders Association was formed in 1965. Whitmore was chairman. Thomopolous, Van der Heuvel and Wetteland represented SA at the world champs in Peru. Harry Bold was editor of the first surfing magazine, *South African Surfer*, which appeared in 1965. It folded three years later, but not before documenting the early days of modern surfing in South Africa.

The first official South African Surfing Championships were held in Durban in 1966. The event was moved from tiny Wedge to Ansteys, which promptly jacked to a solid 12 foot. A triple over-head wave, ridden by non-contestant Neville Callenbourne, was immortalised in a photograph by John Thornton published in *South African Surfer*.

The first official Springbok team was selected from this event, won by McWade. Managed by Whitmore, the SA team competed in San Diego, California. Australian Nat Young won the world title. The team brought back the latest board designs, skills and fashions. They also brought back Van der Heuvel, found wandering around Huntington Beach in a drug haze. He became an instant folk hero as surfers 'tuned in' to rock & roll, 'turned on' to mind-altering substances and 'dropped out', mostly in Jeffrey's Bay, in true 60s style.

A breakthrough for the cold Western Cape came when Gobel imported neoprene from the USA and started making Surf & Ski wetsuits. Zero Wetsuits was born.

Two Australian surfers, John Bachelador and Tony Wright, toured the SA coastline at the end of 1967 riding the revolutionary 'V Machine' boards by Bob McTavish and Nat Young. Suddenly, surfboards over eight feet were obsolete. Nose-riding was history. Square bottom turns, roller coasters and slashing cutbacks were the rage. Boards became shorter and surfers did amazing things on the waves. Surfing changed from riding waves to performing on them.

Derek Jardine with admirer (top) and with mate (above).

Neville Callenbourne – Ansteys, 1966.

It was an era of Jimi Hendrix, Led Zeppelin, Cream and The Doors. Bell-bottom and floral-clad hippies flocked to J–Bay, freaking out the locals. The CIA cited the town as a drug smuggling haven. Some surfers opened Swiss bank accounts to hide the fortunes they accumulated. Durban Poison and Transkei Gold earned a global reputation. Surfing's image plummeted. Older surfers bailed to go fishing, take up golf or other acceptable pastimes. South Africa produced some of the world's best surfers.

In 1969, Wetteland and Ian McDonald staged the Durban 500. The first world champion, Midget Farrelly, competed. Gavin Rudolph won, but it was a financial failure. Peter Burness, secretary of the Natal Surfriders Association, took over and found sponsorship from Gunston cigarettes. The Gunston 500 became the world's longest running professional surfing event, ending 30

The first issue of *Zigzag* magazine.

years later in 1999 when Mr Price took over. In the 70s, Burness invited top surfers to compete in the Gunston to generate overseas invites for South African surfers. Youngsters Anthony Brodowicz, 14, Shaun Tomson, 15, Michael Tomson, 16, Gavin Rudolph, 18, and Errol Hickman were invited to the 1971 Smirnoff Pro Am at Sunset Beach. Rudolph stunned the surfing world by winning in 8–12' surf – in only his second session at the fabled break – becoming the first South African to win an event outside the country

Dozens of foreign surfers competed in Durban, doing the mandatory pilgrimage to Jeffrey's Bay. South Africa became a surfing superpower. Shaun and Michael Tomson joined a global brotherhood including Mark Richards, Rabbit Bartholomew, Buzzy Kerbox, Dane Kealoha and the Bronzed Aussies – Ian Cairns, Peter Townend and Mark Warren.

Other world-class SA surfers were Cape Town's big-wave charger Jonathan Paarman; the king of Jeffrey's Bay, Peers Pittard; PE's Gavin Rudolph; the South Coast's Ant Brodowicz; and Durbanites Mike Esposito, Bruce Jackson, Wayne Shaw and Paul Naude, the first goofy foot to win at Sunset Beach.

In 1976, Naude, Doug McDonald and Mike Larmont started *Zigzag* magazine, which in 1988 was taken over by Craig Sims and in 2001 achieved the milestone of 25 years, making it the 4th oldest surf magazine in the world. Michael Tomson started Gotcha clothing and everybody from Bloemfontein to Alice Springs knew about surfing.

Shaun Tomson won the world title in 1977. A regular visitor to Hawaii with father Ernie and cousin Michael, Shaun

Outer Kom, Cape Town.

South Beach, Durban.

Durban's North Beach, showing the old rock groynes in the foreground.

Wendy Botha - four-time world champion.

Shaun Tomson and the late Peter Burness.

was a seasoned traveller with a clean-cut demeanour and a marketable image. Credited as the world's best tube rider, as immortalised in the movie *Free Ride*, Shaun won six consecutive Gunstons (1973–78). He did more than any other South African to popularise the sport and dispel its drug-related connotations.

Design innovations included Mark Richards's twin-fin in 1978. Spider Murphy started shaping some of the world's best surfboards at Safari in Durban. Lightning Bolt was 'the' label to ride and wear and disco ruled, until punk took over.

In the 80s, apartheid began to hurt South Africans. Visas were hard to obtain for professionals and those wanting to explore exotic destinations.

Everyone was riding twins, including a 14–year–old, Martin Potter, who burst on to the scene, defeating Shaun Tomson in East London on his pro debut and finishing runner-up to Dane Kealoha in the Gunston and Cheyne Horan in the Mainstay Magnum in his first two world tour contests in 1981. East London's Wendy Botha dominated women's surfing. Potter and Botha re-located to Australia. Both won world titles, Potter in 1989 and Botha an incredible four times in 1987, 1989, 1991 and 1992.

Shaun Tomson retired at the end of 1989 after 13 years in the top 16.

In 1983, Ian Cairns introduced the Association of Surfing Professionals (ASP) with surfwear giant OP. South Africa staged four ASP events in 1984, including the Spur Steak Ranch Surf-about in Cape Town and Country Feeling Surf classic at J–Bay. The Spur experienced some of the stormiest weather for an ASP event and J–Bay produced epic 8–12' surf for four days. Young prodigy Mark Occhilupo, 18, won. The next year, the finals of the Spur were held in flawless 15' surf at Outer Kom, the biggest surf for an ASP event outside Hawaii.

Performance surfing took a quantum leap when Simon Anderson introduced the three–fin 'thruster' in 1981. The giant Aussie won events in Sydney slop, four-metre Bells Beach and the Pipeline Masters. South Africans converted in droves.

Floaters were the big manoeuvre in 1985. Pottz and Californian Richie Collins managed to travel unbelievable distances along the 'roof' of the wave before freefalling over the whitewater. Every grommet from Long Beach to Dairy tried to emulate them, sometimes with spectacular results.

In 1986, Paul Botha became the country's first full-time professional surfing promoter, organising the Great Western Cooler Classic in Durban, the inaugural event of the SA Surfing Series (SASS) aimed to provide pro–am events, emulating the ASP tour without the travel costs. Tommy Lawson won. Greg Swart was crowned the first SASS champion after four events.

The decade ended with Craig Sims and Rob van Wieringen taking over *ZigZag*. Steve Morton and David Stolk started *Offshore* magazine in Cape Town and Pat Flanagan started the broadsheet *Wet* in Durban – both publications lasted a couple of years.

Surfing proliferated. Surf shops ope-ned in coastal villages, inland cities and shopping malls. The first wavepool contest was staged at Shareworld in Johannesburg. Only four of the world's top 30 surfers competed in the Gunston 500.

The 90s kicked off with the release of Nelson Mandela. Never a surfer, despite 'hanging out' on wave-rich Robben Island for nearly two decades, the efforts of our master statesman transformed the rest of the world's opinion and South Africans became first-class citizens again.

The ASP introduced their two-tiered world tour structure in 1992. Talks between SASA and the non–racial SA Surfing Union were initiated and a unified amateur body – the United Surfing Council of SA – was formed.

In 1993, the Gunston 500 celebrated its 25th anniversary. The first Ocean Africa festival was staged over 10 days on North Beach and Bay of Plenty. An estimated 250,000 people attended. The concept, devised and coordinated by Peter Burness and Paul Botha, made corporates take notice. The beach lifestyle was booming and surfing was the major attraction.

The SA surfing team was the first to compete under the new national flag at the world champs in Brazil. Paul Canning was the first South African to qualify for the WCT in the ASP's new structure. Sharon Ncongo was the first development surfer to represent SA, in Bali at the grommet champs. Baron Stander opened the Time Warp Museum in Durban.

The 90s were marked by innovations in the Internet, and the improvement of digital weather and wave prediction models. Professor Mark Jury in Zululand and Steve Pike in Cape Town became cyber gurus among hardcore surfers and dabblers alike. Spike's *Wavescape* site and e–mail surf reports showed that technology can benefit all wave riders.

Cass Collier and Ian Armstrong won the ISA big wave world team champs at Todos Santos on their first attempt. The South African surfing industry expanded with a battle for supremacy between local affiliates of multi-nationals Billabong and Quiksilver.

Events such as the WCT-rated Billabong Pro at J-Bay, the Mr Price Pro (successor to the Gunston 500) and the Red Bull Big Wave Africa (a showcase of the country's big wave talent), have kept South African surfing right up there.

Given its colourful heritage and wave-rich coastline that ranges from the powerful cold water surf of the Western Cape to the perfect point-breaks of Eastern Cape to the warm water tubes of KwaZulu Natal, South African surfing has much to be thankful for.

– By Paul Botha

OLD SURF SLANG

Aggressive Surfer – (Surfer who pushes the limits) In the old days, an 'aggressive' surfer 'attacked' the wave, doing moves and pushing the limits of his equipment.

Cover-up – (Tubed) Surfer rides out of sight behind the lip. 'He got a cover-up'.

Drak – (Nasty, horrible or yucky).

Gremmie – (Young, inexperienced or learner surfer) Now known as 'grommets'.

Kraaker – (Big, powerful, good wave) Today a kraaker is a 'cooker'.

Kook – (Derogatory term for 'gremmies') 'You Kooks should go back to Muizenberg / Addington.'

Locked in – (Under the lip but not quite 'covered-up') Riding in the curl of the wave. 'He was locked in.'

Lunch – (Wipe-out) 'Jack was about to get his lunch.'

Pearled – (Nose of the board digs in) 'Chookie caught a kraaker, but pearled when taking off.' The term has since been bastardised. Today a pearler means a perfect wave.

Play – (Classic, great) Another superlative meaning 'great', 'excellent', 'classic' or 'kief'. The remark 'Let's go out, the slides are play,' would be translated as, 'Let's go out, the surf is cooking.'

Rooster trail – (Surfboard wake) Heavier and longer surfboards created a distinct spray. Nowadays, surfers 'draw a line' with lighter, thinner boards.

Skitools – (Baggies) A Cape term for the loose fitting shorts worn while surfing.

Skeg – (Fin).

Slide – (Wave) The wave at St Francis is a 'right slide'.

Soup – (Broken wave or 'white-water') 'The wave closed out and he was left riding the soup.'

Stokey – (Someone who is stoked).

Takes gas – (Wipe-out) More literally, this term referred to a surfer being knocked off his board by the wave.

Too much – (Unreal, radical) Today's equivalent would be 'classic', 'radical' or 'awesome'. That wave was 'too much'.

South Beach surf contest.

Max Wetteland.

There are three main reasons why the surf gets so good in South Africa: good waves; consistent waves; uncrowded waves.

There are hundreds of superb surf spots along our pristine coast, which is 2,798 kilometres long. Peppered with thousands of beaches, bays, river mouths and points, the South African coast boasts many surf spots that would be considered world class, particularly in terms of quality and consistency. Well, we think so anyway. The bonus is that for those with foreign

currency, it's cheap. Millions of people visit South Africa each year with a fistful of dollars or pounds, and come away smiling. If you consider that a beer in a pub will set you back next to nothing, it's not difficult to figure out why.

The main gateway is landlocked Johannesburg, although airlines are constantly launching new direct routes to and from Cape Town, probably the best place to start a trek up the coast in a rented car. If you want a quick-fix surf trip, getting straight to the quality

Morning surf check.

aves without wasting time on the learning
rve, contact one of numerous surf tour
perators who will set you up with a classic
dventure along the coast.

For surfers, South Africa is ideal. Not only
it blessed with a warm climate, it has some
the best and most consistent waves in the
orld. Along the east coast, home to the
stern Cape and Transkei, surfable waves
eak about 200 days of the year.

In winter, it is a rarity for more than a week
go by without head-high waves along the
ast, particularly the Wild Coast of former
anskei, an ethnically rich and fertile region

in the Eastern Cape. Off the coast of the Eastern Cape and KwaZulu-Natal, the continental
shelf comes almost within throwing distance
of the shore.

The continental shelf runs along the edge
of a deep underwater ravine – a sudden drop
in the ocean floor that goes down thousands
of feet. The SW-flowing Agulhas current,
which averages about 6 knots, runs down the
east coast of the country. When it counteracts
the prevailing SW winds, which blow up the
coast, it creates a rippling, upsurge effect
that has sunk big ships.

This oceanographic quirk – coupled with a

constant flow of cold fronts emanating from the South Atlantic – is responsible for a consistency in swell movement and offshore winds almost unparalleled in the world.

Further south, in the southern Cape and Cape Town area, the coast is exposed to the heaving might of the southern Atlantic Ocean, with at least five or six huge swells hitting the coast in winter, reaching twenty feet plus. During winter, frontal storms come past on an almost weekly basis bringing medium to large swells, with consistent 6–8' conditions.

Up north, past the Southern and Eastern Cape, the climate is warm and sub–tropical over the border into KwaZulu-Natal. Classic beachbreaks and occasional points are scattered along a verdant coastal belt of banana trees and palms. This coast has some of the most sublime sand-bar breaks in the world.

But it's not just the surf that brings hordes of surfers to our shores. An intoxicating mix of First and Third World means that when you're driving down an empty road in the veld, with buck and ostrich grazing nearby, you'll think you're in a *National Geographic* wildlife video. But when you hit the next town, a Big Mac or a chilled lager awaits in a friendly rustic tavern.

South Africa is built on the most advanced and efficient infrastructure in Africa with major highways connecting the towns along the coastline. There are 138,000 km of tarred (paved) highways, of which about 2,000 km are expressways. A further 200,000 km are dirt roads.

The Garden Route between Cape Town and Jeffrey's Bay hosts what

Transkei children check out a surfer on his way out of the water.

must rate as one of the best-quality roads in the world. It's a breeze to do the 700 km journey in 6–7 hours.

Dotted along the coast, the surfers will find efficient facilities, beautiful scenery, first-class hotels, excellent restaurants and cheap car hire.

THE ROUTE

If you're flying in, use Cape Town as your entry point to South Africa, either direct or via Johannesburg.

But don't rush off on the search for perfection just yet. Hang out in Cape Town for a while, where you'll find waves on your doorstep. There is an awesome variety of spots in and around the peninsula. The city is within one hour's drive of about 50 breaks, and this excludes numerous spots up the dry, seemingly barren West Coast, as well as spots to the East past Gordon's Bay towards Cape Agulhas (the southern-most tip of Africa).

The West Coast is rich in marine life, and hosts an abundance of surf spots, many undiscovered. Some are accessible by four-wheel drive vehicles only. This coast comprises a few long, winding left-hand pointbreaks, often facing almost North, because they are on the other side of a coastal headland, such as Elands Bay and spots near Saldanha Bay.

The beachbreaks just North of Cape Town can be world class, but can also be fickle and sensitive to wind. The best time of the year is autumn, when light, warm offshores blow and big groundswells begin rolling in from fronts festering in the southern Atlantic.

There are some extraordinary spots

Unnamed spot on the East Coast.

that only work when monstrous storm swells arrive in Cape Town. One spot is aptly called Heaven, although one cannot be sure whether it refers to the quality of the wave, or where you might end up after a brutal wipeout in this powerful, ledging right-hander. A left-hander on the other side of the point is called Hell.

After having your fill of waves, adventure and the laidback lifestyle of one of the world's most beautiful cities, head up the East Coast, either in a rented car or as part of an organised surf tour.

Taking in the breathtaking mountain scenery along the N2 highway, the next main surfing town is Mossel Bay, 3½ hours from Cape Town.

Driving for another 1½ hours, you come to Knysna, home to indigenous forests, elephants, mountains, wild leopard, quaint seaside living and plenty of spots. How far to Jeffrey's Bay? Only two hours.

The Jeffrey's Bay area, incorporating Seal Point, Cape St Francis as well as Jeffrey's, is a surfing mecca with quality waves all over the place, mostly reefs or points, or combinations of the two.

Jeffrey's Bay lies on the southern end of a vast bay, one hour south of Port Elizabeth. The town offers a number of excellent waves, and surprisingly, a number of spots are still secret. When Supertubes is 1–2', and hordes of out–of–towners are scrabbling for waist–high close-outs, the locals are blasting 4–5' walls just around the corner.

Heading North, you arrive at the industrialised city of Port Elizabeth (PE). PE gets windy, with fickle surf spots in Algoa Bay, due to a restricted swell window. However, some city spots fire in the winter, and the city offers good places to stay, with friendly people. The Wild Side, which faces south, gets good in summer because the prevailing NE is offshore there. PE is fairly central if you want to surf the J–Bay area or head up to East London and the Transkei.

PE is near the Addo Elephant Park and other attractions. Visit the 'kief links' section on www.wavescape.co.za for links to a range of South African tourist websites.

Once you're back on the N2, the next main town is Port Alfred, about 1½ hours away. This sleepy hamlet boasts a world-class but fickle right-hander. The coastline up to East London (one hour further north) and beyond, is riddled with ridiculously uncrowded spots, mostly pointbreaks or long sandy beaches with peaks as far as the eye can see.

The East London area is another blessed surf paradise. People who have lived in East London talk of surfing every day for weeks on end. There is an amazing variety of waves in the area, from beachbreaks, rivermouths and pointbreaks to world-class reefs, such as Nahoon, old home to the Gunston 500 (now the Mr Price Pro), the longest running sponsored event on the ASP World Tour.

Just north of East London is the rural Wild Coast, in the former Transkei. It's a rough stretch of coast, rugged and beautiful. Lush green hills undulate across the landscape. Some slope evenly down to the beach, others are cut away, as if chopped by a giant's axe. The jagged cliffs are pounded ceaselessly by wild seas, hence the

West Coast Road towards Cape Town.

Dias Beach staircase, Cape Peninsula.

Wild Coast. Many of the hills are dotted with white mud huts belonging to communities of Xhosa-speaking people. Rivers snake their way through the terrain.

A typical Transkei surf spot comprises a long sandy beach with a headland, or cliffs, at the far end. This outcrop of rocks is the perfect ingredient for a superlative pointbreak. A river often comes out at the base of the point, depositing sand at the point and to the left of the rivermouth.

This combination creates excellent lefthand peaks on the left of the rivermouth, and a long walling wave down the point, often joining up with the rivermouth sand bar and freight-training across the river and on to the beach. Spots like this include Lwandile, Mdumbe and Coffee Bay. Mdumbe can rival Jeffrey's Bay in terms of length and quality.

There are plenty of good waves near Coffee Bay (two hours north of East London) and Port St Johns (two hours north of Coffee Bay).

About another three hours from Port St Johns, still on the N2, you cross the border into sub-tropical KwaZulu-Natal near the seaside town of Port Edward, home to some epic spots, such as St Michaels and many others.

The southern KwaZulu–Natal coast is built up, although there are patches of rural coastline near Hibberdene, where you find a number of awesome little pointbreak setups. One of them is aptly named, The Spot. Befriending a local is likely to be the only way you find this semi-secret spot.

But there are plenty of excellent, easy-to-find beachbreaks scattered along beautiful beaches, fringed by palm trees and banana plantations. Some of the beaches tend to be flatter and often shelve into the sea, making for dumping shorebreaks.

Further north, one passes Warner Beach, home to numerous South African chargers. Inland, sugar cane plantations cover the hilly, verdant terrain. In Durban, the hub of the province, there are numerous world-class waves, including the pier breaks in the city, notably New Pier, an awesome rightander that gets superlative.

Past Durban, and Umhlanga Rocks, you get Ballito Bay and the North Coast. The climate gets hotter and more humid until you're in the tropical zone of Richards Bay and Sodwana Bay. Plenty of secret spots where excellent waves break. This rugged coast is for the adventurous driving 4x4 vehicles only.

CLIMATE

South Africans think of their country as a world in one. The climate can be varied, from hot, dry weather on the West Coast to humid, sub-tropical conditions between East London and the North Coast of KwaZulu-Natal.

The terrain is varied, too, with just about every combination: mountains, deserts, scrubland, savannah, forests and jungle.

South Africa lies in a temperate zone between 22° and 35° South. However, most of the country is elevated, which cools inland areas. Along the coast, weather conditions are moderate, with lesser variations in temperature.

The oceans that surround South Africa determine the climate. The winter cyclones, as discussed in the section on oceanography, bring rain. The cold, north-flowing Benguela Current cools the West Coast, despite hot, desert conditions inland.

The Mozambique and Agulhas ocean currents bring warm water down the coast, generally keeping temperatures higher on the East Coast of the country. The warm, less dense coastal air rises, and lets in rain-bearing clouds brought in by onshore winds from the East.

PEOPLE

You'll find South African people friendly and hospitable. The population of 47 million is made up of a cross-section of cultures. It includes Cape Malays, Afrikaners, indigenous people as well as other settler populations with influences from England, Holland, France, Java, India, China, Scotland,

The aloe, typical of the J–Bay area.

Rural area in the former Transkei on the way to Coffee Bay.

Ireland, Germany and Italy. The population is made up of blacks (75.2%), whites (13.6%), coloureds (8.6%) and Indians (2.6%).

Religions are divided into Christian 68% (most whites and Coloureds, 60% of blacks and 40% of Indians), Muslim 2%, Hindu 1% (60% of Indians), traditional and animistic 28%. There are 11 official languages: Afrikaans, English, Ndebele, Pedi, Sotho, Swazi, Tsonga, Tswana, Venda, Xhosa and Zulu.

FOOD

South African food is generally of a high standard, the ingredients fresh and the cuisine varied and tasty. There is a vast range of eating places, from upmarket restaurants to corner cafés and fast-food joints. There are numerous franchised eateries.

For hungry surfers on the road to the next classic pointbreak, stop off at 24-hour convenience stores. Many of the major convenience stores have spread to South Africa. The main filling stations have a 24-hour shop, with coffee and fast food.

In the urban coastal areas, especially Cape Town and Durban – and to a lesser extent Knysna, Port Elizabeth and East London – there are ethnically diverse bistros and coffee shops offering a cultural melting pot of cuisines.

If your belly is the most important part of your anatomy, notwithstanding other appendages, South Africa is the spot to find the perfect plate of food.

Because of the multicultural nature of its society, South Africa has got just about every type of food on the planet: Malay, Indian, Greek, French, African, pseudo-American, English, Irish, Dutch, Chinese, Thai, Czech, Portuguese, Hungarian, Spanish, Japanese, Italian, Korean and many more.

But perhaps South Africa's most enduring food outlet – the local grocery store or 'kafee' – offers the most value and atmosphere, depending on its owners, who often hail from every corner of the planet, particularly India, China and Greece.

DRINK

If vodka is to Russia, then beer is to South Africa. Millions of litres of the stuff is consumed every day. It's not only because the weather is often hot. Beer is part of the culture, as is biltong, rugby and the braai. The braai is a favourite pastime. You hang out with your mates, grill meat on an open fire, drink cold beer and talk about rugby, or surfing, as the case may be.

South Africa has a wide variety of alcoholic beverages. Its wines are renowned for their quality, particularly the reds. You will find imported (and locally made) Scotch, rum, brandy, port, gin and vodka, as well as locally made stuff like Cane Spirit, Mampoer (a liquor as deadly as Moonshine) and Witblitz ('White Lightning', another vicious homemade spirit). Our wineries also produce their own Grappa, equally as lethal as Mampoer and Witblitz.

Then there is all the exported booze, with ciders, ales and imported English beers.

Recent times have seen the rapid rise of energy drinks and pre-mixed cocktails, with trendy packaging and slick advertising aimed at the so-called Y-generation. Shooters are popular, with pretty girls lurking around beach-

Cape perfection.

side pubs selling single shots of Apple Schnapps and Tequila, among others.

Since apartheid's demise, liquor laws have been considerably relaxed. Nightclubs serve drinks until the early hours. If you like an ice-cold beer after an awesome day's surfing, you won't miss out. In the urban areas, the cities and larger towns offer first-class entertainment, from live music and nightclubs to theme bars and rave clubs. This is apart from numerous rustic music festivals, trance parties and raves for the feral in you.

ACCOMMODATION

In terms of a spot to crash out, a similar variety is offered. Even in the most remote scenic spots of South Africa, there is always a little hotel, caravan park, holiday chalet or campground to chill out in. The management of these establishments along the coast are invariably friendly and accommodating.

Accommodation is affordable, and ranges from backpacker rooms to five-star hotels. There's plenty to choose from inbetween.

OTHER STUFF TO DO

When the surf is flat, a host of adventure sports, safaris and nature trails are available. There is a large range of things to do, from bungee jumping to white water rafting. To get more information, please turn to the useful web resources section on p. 163.

COMMUNICATIONS

The telephone system is the most modern in Africa, with the highest capacity. It consists of digital telephone exchange. The infrastructure is made up of carrier-equipped, open-wire lines, coaxial cables, microwave radio relay links, fibre-optic cable and radiotelephone communication stations. Key centres are Bloemfontein, Cape Town, Durban, Johannesburg, Port Elizabeth, and Pretoria. Communications is run by Telkom, the South African telecommunications giant. Pay telephones as well as card phones are abundant, and local rates are cheap.

RADIO AND TV

There are more than 20 radio stations. Talk radio is popular (Radio 702 and Cape Talk), while music radio caters for all tastes, from Rock and Pop (Eastcoast Radio in Durban and the national 5fm), to jazz (P4 in Cape Town), African soul (Metro FM) and Classical (FMR).

There are a host of regional stations, such as Radio Algoa (Port Elizabeth), Radio Good Hope (Cape Town), KFM (Cape Town), Radio Xhosa (national) and more. Statistics point to an estimated 7.5 million radio listeners (1999). There are five TV channels, three run by the South African Broadcasting Corporation (SABC). E-TV is a private station, while M–Net offers pay-to-view entertainment channels. Many people also have satellite TV, comprising the usual mix of news, education, travel and entertainment.

SEE PAGE 161 FOR TRAVELLER'S FAQS

Surf travellers stop off at a trading store for provisions while on a surf mission in the 'Kei'.

A bodyboarder pulls into a yawning tube at Sandy Bay, which is near Cape Town.

Surfers want to know when they will score that perfect tube. This section provides the tools to achieve that aim by tracking and interpreting weather patterns. It is mostly written for beginners, but seasoned veterans might learn a few things.

There are two things a surfer needs to know about before hitting the beach – wind and swell. Surfers want to know the speed and direction of the wind; and the size and direction of the swell. This will dictate the quality of their surf. With reliable Web-based surf reports, finding out what's happening along the South African coast is easy. However, there is a learning curve involved when it comes to interpreting the data, whether it comes from a barometer, a hand-drawn weather chart or fancy digital model that morphs around on your computer screen.

QUICK GUIDE

It is the air we breathe that creates the waves we surf. Sounds weird, but it's true. Air has weight, which means it exerts downward pressure on the ocean. Some areas contain more air and are denser (high pressure area), while others have less air and are lighter (low pressure area). Meteorologists say that the average pressure over the sea is about 1013 millibars. Areas of low pressure cause storms that can intensify into cyclones. Areas of high pressure are often called anticyclones.

Air in a high pressure area always moves towards a low pressure area. It does this to counteract the imbalance in pressure. When the air starts to move, wind is formed. The bigger the difference in pressure between high and low areas, the stronger the wind. The stronger the wind, the choppier the ocean gets. The choppier the ocean gets, the bigger the swell. The further the swell travels, the better the surf when it breaks!

The distance the wind blows is the

Cyclone swell breaks on the Mound, Durban.

'fetch'. The longer the fetch, the more chance of big, deep swells forming. This is why open oceans get bigger swells than lakes. Most land-locked lakes are not wide enough for the creation of groundswell. These deep, long-travelling swells glide across the ocean in groups or 'sets' of between 5 and 13. They are the surfer's holy grail because, by the time they finally reach shore, the waves are clean and lined up, with regular intervals between each wave, and a lull between each set.

READING THE WEATHER

If you know where high and low pressure systems are situated, and can track their movements, you can work out the direction and strength of the wind and the size and direction of the swell.

The barometer has been a vital tool in measuring weather. Without the aid of satellites, seafarers and coastal dwellers relied – many still do – on the barometer as a way of determining weather patterns. The barometer, which reads atmospheric pressure, can detect changes in the weather. If a barometer indicated a rapid drop in air pressure, the needle swung towards the 'stormy' section, and God-fearing folks battened down the hatches. This was because a storm, or intense low pressure cell, was approaching. The

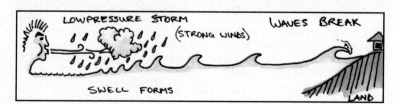

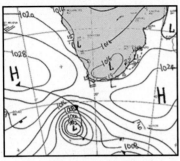

L – Low pressure cell
H – High pressure cell

faster and further the drop in pressure, the worse the weather and the bigger the swell. After the storm, the barometer would indicate an increase in pressure, with the needle rising towards the 'fair' weather section. This meant that the rain would abate, the clouds would clear and the swell would subside.

Although the barometer is a useful tool, it cannot always detect the influence of weather that is far way, particularly the arrival of groundswell formed in the deep ocean. It can only give us readings for local conditions, which are often not influenced by sudden drops in pressure out to sea.

Luckily, we have a tool called the synoptic chart that maps the movement of air pressure over wider areas. You can get updated versions of the South African synoptic chart, whether hand-drawn or computer simulated, from a number of sources on the Web (see p. 163 or visit the Weather section of www.wavescape.co.za). Most daily newspapers carry a printed version.

HOW TO READ A SYNOPTIC CHART

Take a look at the map (left). The snaking contours lines, especially the circular clump, indicate air pressure and the numbers on the lines (isobars), are units of pressure called millibars.

Millibars show the air pressure at that particular point around the pressure system. High pressure cells have a 'higher' number, and low pressure cells have a 'lower' number. The lines are no different to contour lines on a topographical map showing hills or valleys. The closer the lines, the steeper the gradient between areas of high and low pressure.

If you understand the next few paragraphs, the doors of perception will open and all will be revealed.

As discussed, gravity is the reason why air flows from high pressure (heavy air) to low pressure (light air). Gravity exerts its influence by giving weight to air. But there is another powerful force at work – the centrifugal force of the spinning earth. As you know, the earth turns on its own axis, from west to east, creating a continuous, centrifugal force.

In the southern hemisphere, this force causes high and low pressure systems to move in the same direction, from west to east. The force of the rotating earth combined with the efforts of air to move from high to low pressure causes each 'cell' of pressure to spin. Winds blow clockwise around the low and anti–clockwise around the high. It so happens, thanks to those sharp folks at the weather bureau, that this direction is usually the same as the direction of the isobar lines on the synoptic chart. Note, however, that in the northern hemisphere, these forces are mirrored, with pressure systems and winds moving in the opposite direction.

TRACKING PRESSURE CELLS

In the northern hemisphere, a strong low pressure storm is called a typhoon, while in the southern hemisphere, it is called a cyclone. Because of the opposite centrifugal forces between hemispheres of the globe, southern cyclones spin clockwise, tracking from west to east (right). Typhoons do the opposite.

The really big storms off South Africa, often with swells in excess of 60' at their centre, form in the South Atlantic between South Africa and South America. They spin across the Atlantic Ocean, forming in the Roaring Forties to the east of Cape Horn and intensifying as they head east past South Africa, almost like a snowball gathering weight and speed.

In summer, they usually veer away from the southern tip of Africa, plunging into the Antarctic, lessening their effect. Quite often they drop below the country, and continue into the Indian Ocean. A week later the same storm is generating huge waves along the western seaboard of Indonesia and Australia.

However, the storms to watch occur in winter. They get menacingly close to shore, particularly in the Cape Town area. This is the reason the Cape Peninsula is called the Cape of Storms. There have been storms of frightening magnitude, with double hurricane-force

winds, lashing rain and huge, 30' seas.

Occasionally, cyclonic storms form just off our coast, usually to the W or SW of Cape Town. As they move they deepen, but often do not reach the right intensity to create big ground-

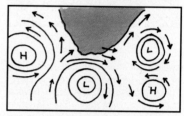

Winds spin clockwise around low pressure

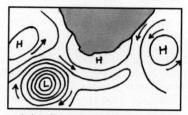

A deep low pressure cell is a cyclone.

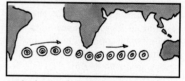

A winter cyclone tracks West to East.

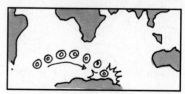

Summer cyclone dips South.

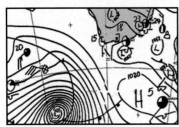
Intense cyclones create huge swell.

THE PERFECT STORM

To look out for groundswell, make sure that your low pressure cell looks like a wad of tightly packed 'tram lines', with a central pressure of 980 mb or less.

The map above shows a very powerful low pressure storm down to a whopping 948 mb at the centre. It's starting to push a 10-15' groundswell towards the SW Cape. If it moves NE, the swell in a few hours, will start jacking to 10' in Cape Town, spreading into the Southern Cape. Notice the number of lines and their tightly packed appearance. Looks like a steep, cone-shaped hill. That's what surfers call serious 'tram lines', or a potent pressure gradient. If you are anywhere near that on a boat, you're looking at the Perfect Storm, and you'd better get the f**k out of there. The alternative is to gibber to the heavens with palms pressed inwards, or hastily run through your emergency procedures. However, if you're sitting under a Milkwood tree on a beach in the southern Cape of South Africa, about 1,500 nautical miles away, start waxing your big-wave gun – a serious swell is about to arrive, without the nasty weather. Despite the fierce storm far out to sea, the weather is mild in Cape Town. The winds on the coast are light and the sea is smooth.

swells until after they have passed out of range, beyond our 'swell window'. These localised storms often have a bark worse than their bite. In other words, they bring the bad weather and cold fronts, but not necessarily the swell.

Be careful with your reading of the synoptic chart. You could be sitting at the beach in stormy conditions, with a flat, messy sea. Occasionally, the swell from these weaker, more localised storms does increase. But it is often ragged and ill-formed, with short wavelengths. Deeper groundswells have longer wavelengths, which means longer intervals between each breaking wave. Storm swell has short intervals, resulting in messy, choppy seas. The swell often disappears quickly too. The weather goes past rapidly, taking the stormy seas with it.

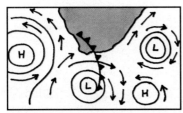
A weak low pressure is not a cyclone. It's just a storm, and it creates less swell

HOW SWELL IS FORMED

When the wind blows, it pushes the water in front of it, transferring energy into the water. Because of the friction between the water and the wind, the water becomes agitated, and begins rolling forwards. The distance over which the wind blows is called the fetch. The longer the fetch and the

A weather satellite image of a cold front as it starts to hit Cape Town.

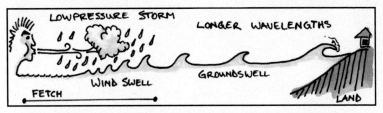

What starts out as windswell, becomes groundswell as it travels across the ocean.

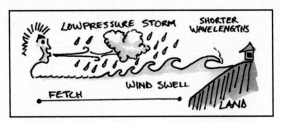

When the storm is closer to land, there is no time for groundswell to form.

stronger the wind, the bigger the swell.

Waves along the South African coast can be divided into two basic types: groundswell and windswell. Groundswell is also created by wind, but with one important difference. windswell is localised chop from a storm. Groundswell is the same localised chop that has been energised and moves faster than the storm, radiating outwards, travelling some distance to reach its destination. The effect is similar to when you hit your rubber duck in your bath to create ripples that lap against the sides.

To be more exact, groundswell is formed by the powerful winds that move in huge circles around a cyclonic storm. The steeper the air pressure gradient, the stronger the winds and the more agitated the ocean becomes. As the sea begins to undulate from the friction of the wind, messy storm swells begin to radiate outwards. At this point, they are still windswells, but as they get bigger and begin to travel further, they become groundswells. Starting out as huge, disorganised lumps, they move through the ocean, slowly losing their ragged edge. The surplus energy is filtered out, and the swells become more organised. Short wavelengths become longer and the swells become more evenly spaced. The swells steadily transform into deep, long swells that travel for thousands of miles.

It should be noted that it is not the water that travels, but rather the energy that transfers itself across the ocean, like a mole burrowing just beneath the surface of the soil. Each groundswell slowly loses size but begins to speed up as it heads away from the storm that created it. If the groundswell has come a long way, it arrives at the coast

as a perfect wall, with enough energy to provide a powerful sliding, tubing motion – the surfer's holy grail. And the reason it arrives on the coast with such superlative form is wavelength.

The longer the wavelength, the further the swell has travelled and the cleaner and more regular it is. However, in recent years, wave buoy readings have enabled researchers to plot an interesting phenomenon.

In Hawaii, it has been noted that buoy readings can show the same size swell, but the wavelength dictates the height of the wave when it breaks. The energy of the swell is more compact and moving faster in a longer wavelength swell. When it breaks, it is bigger and more powerful. That's why we get sudden big swells when it looks like it should be smaller, and vice versa. Satellite and infrared technology are only able to read the swell size, not swell power! A 4' groundswell with peak periods of 23 seconds will jack up a lot more than a 4' groundswell generated close to the coast with a peak period of 14 seconds.

SWELL AND WAVE HEIGHT

There is a difference between the height of the swell as it travels through the ocean and the height of the wave once the swell strikes the land and dumps its load on to the sand. Generally speaking, a four-foot swell results in a wave face between five and eight feet high when it curls, depending on the depth of the water where it breaks. Swell is measured from the back, peak to trough, while wavea are measured from the front, top to bottom.

But there are several other factors, such as the angle of the swell when it hits the reef, the depth of the water over the reef, the speed of the swell, the direction of the wind, the strength of the wind and the length of the peak period between waves (wavelength).

A stiff offshore wind can hold up a swell right until the last minute, mak-

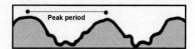

These 6' swells have short wavelengths caused by a nearby storm. Cross-chop between each swell disperses energy unevenly. When the swell breaks at Spot A, the wave face is 10' high.

These 6' swells have longer wavelengths from a distant storm. Energy is more focused, making it more powerful. When the swell breaks at Spot A, it jacks to 12'.

ing the wave stand up higher on the reef. An incredibly shallow reef or sandbar can push more water upwards into the face of the wave, making the face higher than you would think.

There are bizarre exceptions. Check out Teahupoo, the surf spot off Tahiti Sources say the wave never breaks bigger than a wave produced by an 8–10' swell, no matter how big the swell is.

This is a horribly scary phenomenon because the wave, regarded by many as the heaviest in the world, simply gets fatter, thicker and squatter, like a terrifying hump-backed beast.

The speed of the swell and the shalow ledge cause the lip of the curling wave to thicken, rather than pushing the wave face upwards, which most waves do. When a 15' swell hits the reef at Teahupoo, it creates a horrific deep blue step that suddenly convulses, an 8' lip exploding into the impact zone.

Countries have different interpretations of swell height versus wave height. In Hawaii, for example, a 6' foot wave would be seen as an 8–10' wave in, say, the UK. Very roughly, in terms of swell size and wave size, the table below shows the basic difference between the two. Bear in mind that the bigger the swell, the more variable the wave face.

SWELL DIRECTION

In South Africa, the best quality breaks usually face away from the predominant direction of the groundswell, which comes rolling out of the SW or the South. Along the West and East Coasts, swells that come from the southern Atlantic do not strike the coast head-on but travel parallel to the

COMPARING SWELL AND WAVE HEIGHT			
SWELL HEIGHT	METRES	WAVE HEIGHT	FEET
1 foot	¼m	Knee to thigh high	1–2'
2 foot	½m	About waist high	3–4'
3 foot	1m	Waist to head high	5–6'
4 foot	1¼m	Up to 1½ times overhead	6–8'
5 foot	1½m	About 1½ times overhead	8–10'
6 foot	2m	About twice overhead	10–12'
8 foot	2½m	About 2½ times overhead	12–15'
10 foot	3m	About 3 times overhead	15–18'
12 foot	3–4m	3–4 times overhead	18–24'
16 foot	4–5m	4–5 times overhead	24–32'
20 foot	5–6m	5–6 times overhead	32–40'
24 foot	6–7m	6–7 times overhead	40–48'
32 foot	8–9m	8–9 times overhead	50–60'

coast, swinging inwards to break on the shore. Typically, on the East Coast, the northern side of a pointbreak faces N or NE. The prevailing SW swell goes past, with the bigger swells wrapping around the tip of the point, breaking along the rocks.

Because the swell must refract around the headland or point, it is of higher quality, because it only retains its core energy, losing surplus power, filtering out the chop and cleaning up the wave face.

This effect can be seen on a left- or right-breaking point. It also explains why the majority of the best waves up the East Coast are pointbreaks that peel to the right, while the West Coast offers superlative left-hand points.

THE PERFECT WAVE

To recap, swells caused by low pressure storms far out to sea, but with enough intensity (a steep pressure gradient of at least 980 millibars at the centre), are clean and lined up when they arrive at the South African coast. This applies to the Atlantic Ocean cyclones of the south, as well as to the tropical Indian Ocean cyclones to the northeast.

These groundswells arrive in sets of five or more. The sea is calm between waves. When the set arrives, the ocean becomes creased with swell lines. After the set has passed, there is a lull when the ocean returns to a calm state.

A wave's quality is enhanced if the swell must turn, or refract, around a headland or point. This results in a wave of sublime quality and consistency. Jeffrey's Bay and Elands Bay are perfect examples of this effect.

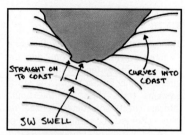

The prevailing swell direction is SW.

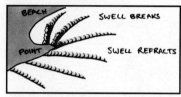

Swells wrap around an East Coast point.

A perfect left breaks on the West Coast.

Jeffrey's Bay fires in 4–6' conditions.

WHY WINTER GETS MORE SWELL

During winter in South Africa, the earth is tilted away from the sun, and the centrifugal forces tend to push the low pressure cells further north. The storm systems track closer to the South African coast, sometimes coming up high enough to actually strike, or scrape past, the coast bringing fierce weather and massive waves.

While these storms bring huge waves, the storm's proximity to the coast results in uneven and messy swell with short, fast wavelengths. The intensity of the storm will obviously depend on the proximity of the low pressure cell. News of a developing cyclone gets surfers excited. In this case, bad weather is good news.

The bad weather comes in the form of cold fronts that accompany cyclonic storms. These huge bands of cloud are swung far to the north like a slingshot from a giant vortex. The stormy conditions emanate from the the epicentre of each storm, and sweep over the land as the low pressure cells move below the country.

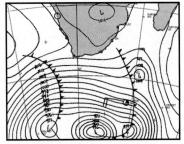

A series of powerful storms move below the coast in winter. The swell keeps on coming.

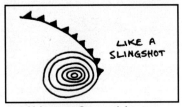

LIKE A SLINGSHOT

Cold fronts are flung north by storms.

NE WINDS

AREA OF WIND SWELL

High pressure causes Easterly windswell.

SUMMER SWELL

In summer, different types of swell come through, particularly up the East Coast. The dominant high pressure system that sits in the Indian Ocean causes NE windswell. The dominant NE winds (SE on the West Coast) can blow for days, agitating the ocean, until a choppy swell begins to break. It is usually messy and lacking in power. However, strong winds out to sea can, like low pressure cells, create powerful waves similar to groundswell.

Areas of low pressure do form off the coast of South Africa in summer, and cold fronts occasionally scrape by, bringing swell and brief periods of offshore winds, particularly along the southern coastal belt and occasionally further up the coast into the Eastern Cape, Wild Coast and KwaZulu-Natal.

Winter swell lines.

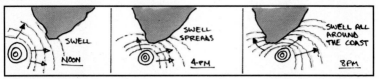

Storm swell spreads east during the day as a low pressure moves rapidly to the East.

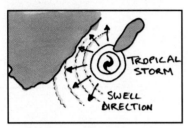

A tropical storm develops into a cyclone.

CYCLONES

These warm ocean storms are smaller than the average Southern Ocean storm. Ranging between 200 and 2,000 km across, they form mostly east of Madagascar in the Indian Ocean, and sometimes track across the island, into the Mozambique Channel. These intensely developed low pressure cells have a warm centre and steep pressure gradients that result in strong winds over the sea. They can bring plenty of groundswell to the KwaZulu–Natal coast, and can reach the Eastern Cape if they track south enough. Bruce's Beauties, the famous wave immortalised in the movie *Endless Summer,* is best on an easterly swell from a tropical cyclone.

A tropical cyclone starts as a tropical depression, with wind speeds of less than 60 km/h. When this reaches between 60 and 110 km/h, it is called a tropical storm. As the winds intensify, speeds begin to exceed 110 km/h. This is when it becomes a cyclone. In the northern hemisphere (North Atlantic and eastern North Pacific) they are referred to as hurricanes. In the western North Pacific they are called typhoons. Cyclones add a new dimension to the northern reaches of the East Coast, particularly KwaZulu-Natal, because cyclones make big waves a possibility in summer, usually the flat season. The cyclone season falls between November and April.

Cyclones are named after people of both sexes, although initially they were only named after women. This was apparently due to the erratic path that cyclones take across the ocean. The last major cyclones in South Africa were Demoina and Imboa, in January and February 1984 respectively. Some surf spots in KwaZulu-Natal only work in cyclone swells. It is when this coast is at its fearsome best. The beauty of riding these huge waves is that, like Hawaii, they can be ridden in boardshorts and nose cream.

GETTING IT RIGHT

Big wave surfers are on the lookout for groundswell, and track the Internet weather maps for signs of the big one. When travelling along our coastline, the trick is to track the weather patterns that will make a difference, especially for the East Coast, which is

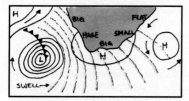

A westerly swell misses the East Coast.

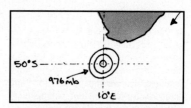

If the low peaks to 976 millibars near or above 50° South and on or East of 10° East, you are almost guaranteed swell along the SW and S Cape coastline.

the most difficult to work out. As a general rule, a low pressure storm passing on or above 50° South and past 10° East needs a pressure of 976 mb at its centre to produce a good swell, certainly for the southern Cape.

Whether this swell reaches up the East Coast to the Eastern Cape and KwaZulu-Natal depends on the speed, angle and intensity of the storm, and whether it holds its line as it goes past. If it stays high enough, it will push swell up and around the East Coast as it starts turning a 'corner' at Cape St Francis. At this point, instead of running from W to E, the coastline begins to head NE. If the storm prematurely fades, or falls to the S or SE, the swell comes out of the W, and misses the East Coast.

This is also a possible explanation as to why Seal Point (SE tip of SA) is so consistent. It is one of the last exposed spots on the southern coast. A westerly groundswell can be huge in the Western Cape, but flat along the Eastern Cape, despite huge lumps on the horizon. When a westerly swell is running, you can be sitting at your favourite spot, amped to go, but the huge lumps you see sliding past on the horizon are not breaking along the shore. That's because the swell is too westerly, and is going straight past.

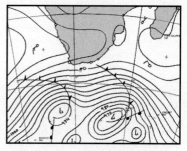

The East Coast gets solid groundswell from a low pressure storm that has maintained a more easterly trajectory.

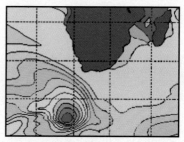

Swell model shows swell size. The storm is at its peak. A big swell is about to hit Cape Town, but it will miss the East Coast.

RESOURCES

If the learning curve is too much for you, and time is short, check out a variety of sources for surfing information. Technology has brought huge changes to weather prediction and analysis. Surfers are not complaining, although some purists cry foul.

Check out the Wavescape Surf Report and Weather section, a portal to weather, wind and swell resources, including US Navy swell models, academic databases, current wind readings, satellite pictures, regional surf lines, synoptic charts, interactive data charts, and animated GIFs that indicate a range of swell, wind and weather data: www.wavescape.co.za.

Here you will find access to models and maps generated by the Climate System Analysis Group, part of the Environmental and Geographical Science Department at the University of Cape Town. This excellent resource can be found at www.egs.uct.ac.za/csag. There are also a number of other useful services, which are provided to the public by the South African Weather Services: www.weathersa.co.za.

OFFSHORE AND ONSHORE WINDS

Generally, coastal winds in South Africa blow in cycles according to the interplay between the areas of low and high pressure that pass from west to east.

When a low pressure cell approaches, the first wind to blow is generally N or NW. This wind is mostly onshore on the West Coast because it blows from the sea and mostly offshore on the East Coast because it blows from the land. And, as any discerning surfer knows, onshore winds are no good for surfing, unless you're desperate, because the ocean gets all mushy and the swells are uneven and messy. But when the wind blows into the sea from the land, it cleans up the texture of the ocean, pushing up the face of the waves and making them more orderly.

When the cold front has passed over the southern coastal belt, the NW winds there also swing to SW. During a cold front, the southwester is particularly strong along the SE tip of the country, often for some days on either side of the storm. Port Elizabeth is situated in this area. It is not called the 'Windy City' for nothing. The effect the cold front has on the Eastern Cape and into KwaZulu–Natal depends on the strength and proximity of the low pressure cell behind the bad weather. Sometimes the cold front misses these parts of the coast completely. Sometimes the entire country is hit by severe winds. It all depends. But once the cold front has passed and the storm is careening across the Indian Ocean on its way to Australia, the swell subsides.

Then the other half of the cycle comes into play: the high pressure system. High pressure cells do not move in the way that cyclonic storms do. They kind of creep in behind the cold front, filling the 'hole' left by the passage of the storm. In Cape Town, for instance, the Atlantic High 'ridges in' against the land in the wake of the front, causing the winds to swing to the east or southeast. The strength of the southeaster, which howls for days on end in summer, depends on the speed with which the High ridges in, as well as its intensity.

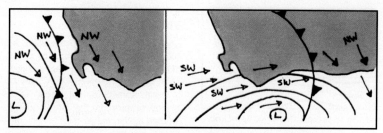

The NW moves ahead of the approaching front, followed by fresh SW winds.

Once the high moves in from the west, it often splits in two, with one half in the Atlantic bringing strong SE winds to the Western Cape area, and the other half in the Indian bringing strong NE onshore winds to the coast. This is when everyone goes back to their day jobs, and forgets about surfing for a while because conditions are lousy.

TRANSITIONAL WINDS

There are two transitional winds, or 'on-the-cusp' winds: the northerly and the southerly. These blow between the influence of the high or low pressure systems, when one is about to start dominating the other.

For the northerly winds, imagine that the Low and High are two cogs turning into each other. The left cog spins clockwise while the right cog spins anti-clockwise.

Between them the flow pulls downwards, a northerly flow (see p. 48).

This effect often occurs when a high pressure cell is moving off to the east, and a low pressure is approaching from the west. The more acute the pressure gradient between the two systems, the stronger the wind.

Southerly winds generally occur when the low pressure cell has gone, the cold front has passed and the high is about to ridge in behind it. This has the opposite effect. In other words, the anti-clockwise high turns outward with the clockwise low, creating an upward flow, or southerly (see p. 48).

As the front arrives, it's NW. As the front moves up coast, it's SW. The wind then goes SE.

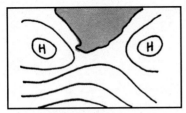

SE on West Coast, NE on the East Coast.

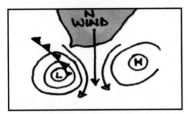

As the low approaches, the North wind blows between the two weather systems.

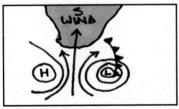

As the high ridges, the wind turns southerly.

A WINTER CYCLE IN THE EASTERN CAPE

Cool in the morning with no wind. As the sun climbs, it warms up. The sea is like glass, with a clean 3–4' ground-swell running. The temperature rises as a warm, sometimes hot, 'berg' wind begins to blow in the late morning, feathering the waves into perfect off-shore textures. Temperatures reach almost 30°C. By evening, a few 4–5' sets are breaking.

The next day, the morning starts with a warm offshore breeze. It's starting to get cloudy. The breeze slowly swings from berg wind to SW and picks up to a moderate wind, which cools down the air temperature. The swell gets bigger.

By the third day, the southwesterly is a stiff breeze and it's cooler, the clouds are scudding across the sky and the swell is grinding away at 10'. By afternoon, the wind is howling SW.

For the next two or three days, the weather remains the same, with intermittent rain and patches of sun. Once the swell has peaked, it begins to drop off again and the cycle starts with new storms forming in the south.

Kalk Bay in winter.

Clean swell along Noordhoek Beach, Cape Peninsula.

Cyclone swell at Wedge, Durban.

A WEATHER SEQUENCE

The following sequence is typical of the passage of weather systems in South Africa, whether in summer or winter. This sequence takes place in summer, because the arrival and departure of the cold front and passage of low pressure cell is swift. In winter, low pressure cells are more frequent and more dominant, keeping the high pressure cells at bay for longer periods. In summer, a cold front is normally an isolated event, whereas in winter, cold fronts can arrive one after the other, with synoptic maps showing low pressure cells like pearls strung together on a necklace.

DAY 1 – The country is sandwiched between two high pressure cells, in the Atlantic and Indian Oceans. Winds in KwaZulu-Natal are onshore NE. There is scattered rain on the East Coast as moisture-bearing wind blows from the sea. The NE wind along the SE coast (Port Elizabeth to East London) is swinging and a warm N–NW berg wind is developing, blowing off the land. On the Cape Peninsula, a strong SE is keeping the weather hot and dry. A 2–3' swell is running along the Southern Cape in glassy N conditions. The NE onshore in KZN is making the 1–2' swell mushy and blown out, although the day started with a light glassy NW offshore.

DAY 2 – The approaching low pressure cell begins to push the Atlantic High out of the way. The SE flow on the West Coast backs off, and the wind drops. A light NW breeze starts in the SW Cape. High cloud appears in Cape Town. The swell shows signs of increasing – from 3' to 5' in Cape Town – as the pressure drops. No effect is felt in the Eastern Cape or in KZN, although the berg wind along the SE coast has freshened and the weather is not as humid. Some clean offshore 2' sets are breaking in the East London area. Durban is fresh NE, but with a Northerly tinge to a humid onshore. It's raining in northern KZN. The swell in KZN is still a mushy 1–2'.

DAY 3 – The front strikes Cape Town and sweeps up coast. A thick band of dense cloud and rainsqualls moves east. The NW breeze in Cape Town increases to 30 knots, then swings to SW. It's mushy and onshore along the Atlantic side, with solid 8' sets. The NW berg wind on the East Coast dies, and cooler, fresh SW breeze pushes up

the coast, strong in Port Elizabeth. It arrives in Durban in the late afternoon. The low intensifies as it passes. The swell in the Eastern Cape goes from 4' to 10'. J–Bay is a perfect 4–6' in clean offshore conditions. The swell pushes into KZN, with the South Coast firing in the afternoon, up to 6' at St Mikes, and up to 4' in Durban.

DAY 4 – The front begins to move away. The weather in KwaZulu-Natal is still rainy and a SW wind is still blowing in the Eastern Cape. Epic conditions continue between East London and Durban, but the wind is swinging to the south along the southern Cape as the Atlantic High moves into the void left by the low pressure. As the high pressure ridges against the SW Cape and West Coast, the wind in Cape Town rapidly swings from SW to S, and the weather clears. By evening, the SE is back, howling. The only cloud left is the tablecloth on Table Mountain. A ragged 4–6' swell is dropping fast.

DAY 5 – The swell subsides and the High pressure asserts its dominance once again. In Cape Town, the swell is 2–3' and there are some pea-green barrels along the open beachbreaks on the Atlantic side. However, by lunchtime the ferocious Southeaster has obliterated the swell, and the sea has gone flat. Meanwhile, the onshores have spread all the way up the East Coast, with SE onshore winds blowing along the entire coastline, turning a dropping 4–5' swell into mushy lumps. The high moves east, still trying to follow the fading low pressure cell, and starts breaking up.

DAY 6 – The cycle is complete and we're back to square one, with the SE pumping in Cape Town, and the high divided into two entities, one off the East Coast, and the other ruling to the west of Cape Town. The swell has gone and the seas have returned to their normal summer state, a mushy 2–3' on the East Coast in fresh NE onshore winds, and an icy, wind-whipped 1–2' along the Cape Peninsula in galeforce SE winds, depending on the strength of the Atlantic High. In the Southern Cape, a moderate to fresh E wind is blowing and the swell is 2–3'. A new low pressure cell builds in the South and the next front approaches. Looks like this one will arrive in three days.

The main features of South Africa's oceanographic makeup are the continental shelf, which lies off the East Coast of the country, and three mainstream currents: the Mozambique, Agulhas and Benguela currents. The first two flow down the East Coast of the country, while the icy Benguela flows up the West Coast.

MOZAMBIQUE CURRENT

This is a warm current driven by SE trade winds toward the east coast of Africa. Because of the earth's rotation, it is directed south, following the mainland and the continental shelf. Part of the flow passes east of Madagascar. The rest heads West and down through the Mozambique Channel, influencing the climate of KwaZulu-Natal. Both streams join the Agulhas Current that flows down towards the Cape. The Mozambique Current is warm, between 18° and 28° C.

AGULHAS CURRENT

This current flows down the East Coast and veers eastward to join the flow from Africa to Australia. Some of the flow continues westward around the Cape of Good Hope into the Atlantic. The Mozambique Current also feeds the Agulhas Current. Only 60 nautical miles wide, the Agulhas Current flows up to 5 knots off the southeast coast of South Africa, roughly around the Transkei and East London, making it one of the fastest-flowing currents in the world. The Agulhas Current is warmish, between 14° and 26° C.

BENGUELA CURRENT

The cold Benguela moves up the West Coast of South Africa from the Southern Ocean around Antarctica.

The confluence of the Benguela and the warm Agulhas occurs somewhere between Cape Point and Cape Agulhas. The water just off the West Coast of South Africa is rich in plankton and other nutrients, which is why the West Coast, including the coast of Namibia, is so rich in marine life. The Benguela is cold, ranging from 8° to 16° C.

CONTINENTAL SHELF

The width of the continental shelf – a submerged platform that extends from all the continents – varies around southern Africa. From the coast, the shelf drops gradually to between 200 and 300 m, then drops vertically into the abyss.

Along the eastern seaboard the drop is found close to the shore. Along parts of the Transkei Wild Coast, the shelf is only 10 km away. This infamous coastline has seen many ships sunk by freak waves and huge seas.

Several unique ingredients combine to create swells up to 60' high. Mostly in winter, galeforce southwesters work up the seas, creating localised swells with short wavelengths that travel into the oncoming Agulhas current, flowing south off the shelf. This increases the size of each wave. However, a freak wave only occurs when these waves merge with deep storm swells from the south. These long wavelength swells, travel thousands of miles from potent westerly storms in the south. Such freak waves have sunk ships, some without trace. Not surprisingly, the Wild Coast is known as one of the world's most treacherous stretches of coast. For surfers, naturally, it's a paradise.

Along the southern Cape and West Coast, the shelf's decline is more gradual. Off Cape Agulhas, Africa's southern-most tip, the 200 m contour is 270 km from the shore. Off the West Coast, it's about 200km at the mouth of the Orange River. Off Cape Town, the shelf comes to within about 80 km.

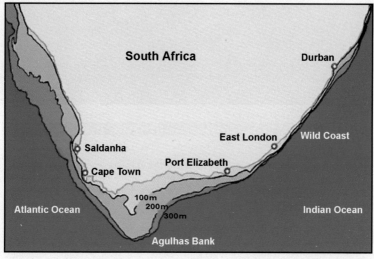

Map showing the contours of the continental shelf. The shelf comes closest to shore off the East Coast, especially Transkei and the northern KwaZulu-Natal coast.

Zambezi shark

DON'T BE A WUSS

The reality about sharks has been clouded by paranoia. Much of the fear of sharks is without substance, although certain precautions should be taken when surfing in South Africa. After all, the ocean is suited more for fish than humans.

However, surfers, unlike your regular landlubber, tend to take chances. They push their luck by surfing when there are shoals of fish around, such as sardines or mullet, or when floodwater from rivers deposits organic material in the sea, making the water brown and murky. This is a frequent occurrence in the Transkei and KwaZulu-Natal, when summer rains swell the rivers.

Some South African surfers ignore bleeding cuts, and continue surfing. The author has been guilty of this when surfing in the Transkei. In our youth, we would often carry on surfing after seeing a shark. Once it happened in the Transkei when a large hammerhead cruised past. Another time, we watched fishermen catch a two-metre ragged tooth shark off the East Pier, Port Alfred, during a heat in a university surfing competition.

Some sharks, particularly the Great White, are seen as killing machines, blindly and constantly on the hunt for blood. This is not necessarily true. They are generally elusive, wary and selective in their hunting habits.

South Africa is home to a number of species that have been known to attack people. The bulk of attacks come from the Ragged Tooth, Tiger, Zambezi, Hammerhead and Great White sharks. However, it is the 'unholy trinity' of the Tiger, Zambezi (Bull) and Great White that make up the majority of attacks on humans.

It must be stressed, however, that surfing is a safe sport in South Africa,

Ragged tooth shark

especially if the right precautions are taken.

For the Great White, perhaps the most maligned of the shark species, there is an abundance of prey. The Great White feeds mostly off huge colonies of Cape fur seals, which number in the hundreds of thousands off the Cape coast.

Remember, the number of shark attacks are relatively low – you have far more chance of being killed by a falling coconut in Thailand than being killed by a shark in South Africa, so don't get all wussie about going surfing. For more information about sharks, check out this website: www.ocean-star.com/shark.

South Africa recognises the value that Great Whites play in our ecosystem. The species, which came close to being endangered a few years ago, is protected by law. South Africa pioneered an international convention to protect Great Whites from attack by humans.

MYTHS

There are a number of myths about sharks that need to be straightened out. Sharks don't especially like the taste of us humans. In fact, they try and avoid us where possible. People are not their normal prey. Most shark attacks on surfers occur as a result of mistaken identity with seals. In most cases, a shark will back off after realising its mistake. Sadly, the damage done to the victim during the initial hit can – in rare cases – be fatal.

A common perception is that sharks are stupid. However, it has been proven that they are complex creatures that can even be trained.

Many people also think that sharks

are virtually blind, but have sensitive hearing and sonar capabilities to detect prey. While sharks are sensitive to noise – they can detect potential prey thrashing about in the water – this is a fallacy. Sharks see different colours, and have good eyesight, often many times more sensitive to light than human eyes. The Great White uses sight as the primary means to 'lock on' for an attack.

Sharks are not scavengers or feeding machines constantly hunting for food. Most sharks have specific diets. Great Whites, for instance, generally prefer seals, some sharks eat plankton, others snack on fish.

In the False Bay area of South Africa, Great White sharks have been known to exhibit similar patterns to Killer Whales. When attacking a seal, they have been known to strike their victim from beneath, hitting the hapless mammal into the air. On its way down, the seal is caught in the convulsing jaws of the shark. The Great White has the ability to protrude its jaws, giving it more elasticity when devouring prey. During the chase, Great Whites often leap into the air, as does the Mako shark.

ATTACKS

Yes, there have been shark attacks in South African waters. With the introduction of nets, the number of attacks decreased dramatically in KwaZulu-Natal, a traditional hunting ground for the Zambezi and Tiger sharks, two of the most lively marine predators.

Spots with the most shark attacks, include: Ntlonyane (Transkei), Nahoon Reef (East London), Fish Boma (Knys-na), Igoda Mouth (East London), Gonubie Point (East London), Amanzimtoti (southern KwaZulu-Natal), Gansbaai (near Hermanus) and Keurbooms (near Plettenberg Bay).

PLAY IT SAFE

To reduce the rare chance of attack, follow these simple rules:

– don't surf at dawn or dusk
– don't surf near river mouths in flood
– don't piss in your wetsuit
– don't surf with a bleeding wound.

Timing is another factor when surfing the East Coast of the country. The best times of the year are autumn, winter and early spring, between March and October. The summer months are hot and humid, with a lot of rain, which makes the water more attractive to sharks.

MAIN 'MANEATERS'

Bull or Zambezi Shark
Carcharhinus leucas
The Zambezi is much smaller than the Great White or Tiger – up to three metres long. It's a heavy looking fish – hence the name Bull – and accounts for many attacks in KwaZulu-Natal and Transkei. Common in warm seas, especially around river mouths, it travels up rivers looking for food. When the Transkei rivers are in flood, cows and other animals drown and are washed downstream.

Apparently, Zambezi sharks have been found 3700 km up the Amazon, as well as up the Zambezi in Zimbabwe. An opportunistic feeder, the Zambezi often attacks without reason.

Tiger Shark
Galeocerdo cuvier
Perhaps the most dangerous shark, it lives in tropical waters. Common off the coast of KwaZulu-Natal. Grows big, up to six metres long. Not as discerning as the Great White. When it attacks, it keeps going with particular voracity. Has been known to bite or bump boats.

Great White Shark
Carcharondon carcharias
Grows up to six metres long. Second to the Killer Whale as a marine predator. Feeds on seals. Found off the waters of the Cape. Nomadic, elusive and wary fish. Known to breach while chasing prey. A beautiful prehistoric beast that is officially protected in South Africa.

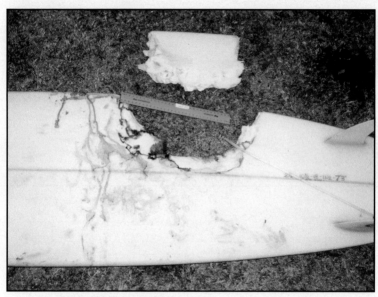

A case of mistaken identity is not going to provide much comfort.

SURF SPOTS
& THEIR RATINGS

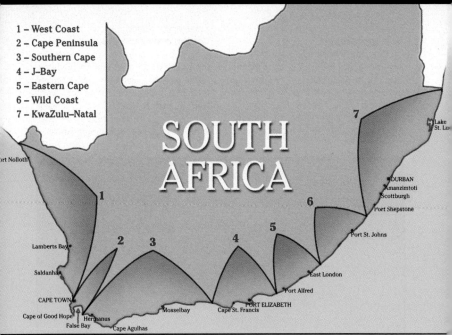

1 – West Coast
2 – Cape Peninsula
3 – Southern Cape
4 – J-Bay
5 – Eastern Cape
6 – Wild Coast
7 – KwaZulu–Natal

SOUTH AFRICA

ort Nolloth

Lake St. Lu

DURBAN
Amanzimtoti
Scottburgh
Port Shepstone

Port St. Johns

Lamberts Bay

Saldanha

East London

CAPE TOWN

Port Alfred

Cape of Good Hope
False Bay
Cape Agulhas

Hermanus

Mosselbay

PORT ELIZABETH
Cape St. Francis

SURF SPOTS

The surf spots are detailed from west to east, starting from the mouth of the Orange River, down through the West Coast, and down to Cape Town. The Mother City lies on a peninsula that boasts an incredible 50 breaks within an hour's drive. Then east along the southern Cape, past Jeffrey's Bay, home to superlative reefs and points. Then it's on to the Eastern Cape, offering a classic variety of points, beaches and reefs. After that, we head up the rugged coastline of the Wild Coast. Heading further north, the climate becomes increasingly warmer until we hit the subtropical region of KwaZulu-Natal.

RATINGS

Each spot gets a star rating, based on experience (which is opinion) and heresay ('You should have been here yesterday').

★★★★★ This wave is awesome. World class in power, form and length of ride, with a couple of exceptions when sheer perfection makes up for the shorter ride. Highly recommended.

★★★★ The four-star wave is classic. It's also high on adrenal capability, but may fall slightly short on form, consistency or length. It's very rideable and offers power sections. Recommended.

The East Coast is characterised by right-handers.

★★★ The three-star wave is fun, with hotdog sections and a bit of juice here and there. It might be unknown, potentially offering conditions that are better than expected. A fun wave.

★★ Generally a weak, or inconsistent break. Mostly suitable for beginners, but not really recommended for those seeking some 'juice'.

★ A wave lacking any real power, size or form. This wave is not going to prompt an overflow of adrenalin, but it should provide some fun for beginners.

OTHER SYMBOLS

Each surf spot has symbols representing what the average sea temperature is, whether the spot is rock or sand bottom and the skill required to surf the break whether it be beginner, intermediate or experienced. The symbols are as follows:

Sea temperature from ± 10°C ————

Up to ± 25°C ————

Sand bottom————

Rock bottom————

Suited for beginners————●

Intermediate surfers ————■

Experienced surfers————◆

WEST COAST

T his stretch of coast looks dry and barren. But it is one of the most nutrient-rich areas in the world. It teems with sea life, fed by plankton and nutrients upwelled from the deep water.

The water is coldish all year around, due to the attentions of the icy Benguela Current, but does get warmer in winter around Cape Town because the Southeaster stops blowing, which means the warmer surface water stops getting blown out to sea. The sea temperature varies between 11 and 20 degress Celcius. Characterised by long white beaches and rocky outcrops, or points, there are several peninsulas, or large hook-shaped headlands. In several instances, the best waves are on the north-facing

Elands Bay.

side of these headlands. Good for long left-hand pointbreaks, such as Elands Bay.

The land hosts a range of fascinating plants, particularly the bizarre array of succulent semi-desert plants. It comes alive in spring when millions upon millions of flowers blossom to carpet the earth in a myriad colours. In terms of surf, there is plenty of choice. The best conditions occur when a strong groundswell pushes up from the south before a cold front, the weather is still clear and the wind pattern has locked on to a warm northeasterly berg wind, the precursor to a swing to the northwest as the front approaches. This makes for big clean waves textured into glassy perfection by the offshore winds.

PARADISE **** ■ ⌂

Paradise is a right pointbreak that works on a smaller swell than Samson's Bak. Runs along rocks on the inside after a re-form wedges over a rocky ledge.

SAMSON'S BAK ***** ♦ ⌂

A powerful right-hand pointbreak that delivers some epic waves when conditions are right: a solid 6–8' groundswell, light offshore and pushing tide. Kelpy and cold.

TRAILER BAY **** ♦ ⌂

Trailer Bay is a similar set up to Elands Bay, without the crowds. It walls up to give a freight train ride. Gets pretty scary because it walls up over a solid block of rock, then swings outward and into a small bay.

NAMAQUALAND ***** ■ ⌁ ⌂

This vast expanse of semi-desert is a paradise for fleshy desert succulents. There are numerous surf spots, but you will need a four-wheel drive, lots of provisions and some local knowledge. Word has it that several secret spots deliver epic surf.

STRANDFONTEIN *** ■ ⌁

Fun but fickle right-hand beachbreak. Sandbanks shift around a lot in rippy conditions. Best in calm or berg winds during a small to medium swell and incoming tide.

ELANDS MAGIC...ELANDS MAGIC...ELANDS MAGIC...ELANDS

ELANDS MAGIC

By Will Bendix

It's natural, part of the learning curve. The older and better at something you get, the higher you set your standards and the greater your goals become.

Like learning to stand on a surfboard. At first you're awed by the fact that you can stand and ride straight, propelled by the motion of the ocean. Then pumping that little foamie becomes standard procedure. Actually riding with the swell becomes the next big thing. Before you know it, carving and cutbacks become part of the repertoire and the rest, as they say, is history.

The same goes for surf spots. When I began surfing, a train ride to Muizenberg near Cape Town with my connections was my idea of an exotic surf journey, fraught with dangers and adventure – like trying not to get bust by the conductor – only to arrive at that Nirvana of beginners surfing, 'The Berg'. We would sit out at the backline hooting randomly as lumpy little swells

DORING BAY ★★★★ ▪ ♛

Left reef break. There is an inside section that runs along rocks. Needs a light SE wind or glassy easterly winds. Best on a clean 4–6' groundswell.

DONKIN BAY ★★★ ▪ ♛

Left pointbreak. Needs a solid 10' + storm swell, preferably in winter. A reef on the outside blocks off much of the force. Like Elands, it copes with SW winds. Works on a low tide. Likely to be working if Elands is out of control.

LAMBERT'S BAY ★★ ● ▭

In front of the river mouth, near the caravan park, are sandbanks that offer some waves on the low tide. Best in a light wind with a moderate swell.

GARBAGE DUMPS ★★★★ ▪ ♛

There are two waves named Garbage Dumps Rights and Lefts. The right is a pointbreak with slow moving walls. The left is also a pointbreak, best on the low tide. The ride ends in front of a rocky shelf. East winds are offshore and it therefore needs a biggish swell before it works. Lots of kelp around.

FARMER BURGERS ★★★★ ▪ ♛

A rocky shelf just south of Lambert's Bay produces a fun, sometimes classic 2–5' wave, as long as conditions are glassy or a NE berg wind is blowing. So named after a nearby farmer called, you guessed it, Mr Burger, a legend in the area.

...ELANDS MAGIC...ELANDS MAGIC...ELANDS MAGIC...ELAN

struggled lethargically by. I'd grin to myself and think of how the Camel man had nothing on us.

Gradually, we lost our taste for the Berg and moved on to bluer pastures, hitching to Long Beach or Witsands, and sometimes convincing a poor parent to sacrifice their car and sanity to take a bunch of screaming pubescents to exotic locations such as Llandudno or 'gasp' Koeëlbay, an hour from home base. Around this stage, somewhere before drivers licences and long before thoughts of overseas, we planned

the trip of all trips. It was to be an expedition for more than two hours up the West Coast to Elands Bay, about as foreign as we could imagine.

The glinting lefts of E–Bay lured us like a flock of zombie magpies.

Somehow we convinced my older sister and her friend (who had a licence) that it would be a good idea for them to take our posse of seven crusty teenage kids up for the weekend in my mom's old yellow Kombi. Van loaded to the hilt, we all skipped school early one Friday to set out

ELANDS BAY ★★★★★ ■

The J–Bay of the West Coast. In the right conditions, this wave gets classic. A rocky, kelp covered shelf, or small point, which turns a corner and becomes sand at a small river mouth. The swell refracts around the outer area of Elands Bay and peaks at the point, producing a hollow take-off and cylindrical wall that runs for about 150 metres. Needs a solid SW swell of 8' before it wraps around the point. If Cape Town is a solid 6–8', and the northern suburbs are 3–4', chances are Elands will be 3–5'. Handles any S wind. Dominant wind is SE.

STOMPNEUS ★★★★ ■

Another West Coast left-hander. It's a point that needs a strong SW swell to wrap around the rocks, giving enough juice to turn on the inside bowl, which faces due North. It easily handles a SW wind, and needs a mid to high tide. Best in huge winter groundswells (10–20') and southerly winds. There is an outside reef that prefers a low tide. Also requires a solid swell, but more exposed.

PASTURES ★★★★ ●

On the northern side of a headland called Shelly Point, north of Saldanha Bay. This place gets good, but not all that often. A pointy left-hander that needs a huge ocean swell for it to start breaking. Offshore winds are SW-SE. Lots of fun. A mellow pointbreak. Fickle.

HELL ★★★ ◆

The wild side of the spot called Heaven. A bit wild and rocky, but gets good in SE or SW winds.

ELANDS MAGIC...ELANDS MAGIC...ELANDS MAGIC...ELANDS

---

on what would surely be a pioneering expedition into the realm of hardcore adventure – after we got mom's permission.

Leaving Cape Town, the West Coast road coiled ahead like a lazy serpent, occasionally twisting close enough to reveal a shimmering Atlantic ocean creased by bumps of swell and smears of whitewash. This would always ensure an explosion of hoots, squeals and inevitably somebody getting the crap punched out of them as the old battered VW shuddered to contain so much energy. Ahead of us loomed the holy Mecca of Elands Bay, and soon the coastal fynbos gave way to open, barren stretches of landscape, punctuated by rising hills and lonely farmhouses. Once the coast was out of sight, the conversation wavered from surfing to equally exaggerated stories about 'scoring with chicks' and charming facts such as who hadn't washed their hair for the longest. My sister's friend just shook her head as she drove and probably wondered how the hell she had been conned into this. To us, this weird, art student hippie chick was as

West Coast kelp.

Kelp and seaweed

There more than 800 species in our waters, making South Africa one of the richest marine flora environments in the world. There are three main regions from the tropical Indian Ocean of northern Kwazulu-Natal to the prolific kelp beds along the West Coast. The Southern Cape coast, with the West Coast, is a temperate zone. The 150 km coastline of the Cape Peninsula alone hosts more than 350 kelp and seaweed species. For surfers, tubular kelp beds in the cold waters of the Cape can be an irritation, especially when a surge maroons you on a clump of kelp heads, where you flail like a horny tortoise. But they are rich in nutrients, supply oxygen to the water and host a plethora of sea creatures in their fronds. South Africa's seaweed industry involves the sustainable harvesting of two main resources: kelp and the red seaweeds which are found in warmer water up the East Coast.

Red tides

Caused by the rapid population explosion of single-cell phytoplankton known as *dinoflagellates*, red tides can be harmful to sea life and other creatures. In the right conditions, these organisms can replicate to as many as 60 million cells per litre.

Red tide is not always red. Dis-

colourations can be brown, orange or purple. One of the worst cases of red tide in South Africa occurred in 1994 up the West Coast, when 60 tons of crayfish and 1,500 tons of fish washed ashore in the St Helena Bay area.

Red tides often occur in autumn or late summer, usually along the southern and Western Cape. They are caused when prevailing southeasterly winds cause upwelling. The ocean floor is stirred up and nutrient-rich sediment rises towards the surface. When the right nutrients combine with the correct temperature, salinity and light, the dormant *dinoflagellates* grow with amazing speed, like sea atoms splitting. It has been noted that several other factors assist their proliferation, such as increased levels of trace metals and pollution. The density of a red tide is determined by currents, tides and the way the organisms swim to the surface using two whip-like appendages called flagella.

Red tide can be harmful in numerous ways. The event can deplete the water of oxygen, which leads to the mass mortality of sea life. When shellfish consume *dinoflagellates*, neurotoxins can collect in their tissue. This can cause paralytic poisoning of predators, including humans who feed on the shellfish. The excretion of neurotoxins into the sea can also cause skin irritations.

HEAVEN  ★★★★★ ◆ 👑 ⬛

Befriend a local to take you there as a special guest. Otherwise you won't find it. When a raging 15–20' storm swell is pummelling the Cape Peninsula just before or after a cold front has passed, Cape Town surfers say 'Let's go to Heaven'. This small rock bottomed reef / point will be in the 6'+ range. A kelpy foamy cauldron of Atlantic juice, Heaven throws up a thick-lipped wall for about 80 metres, with a stomach-churning bowl section halfway down. Not for the faint hearted. Best in glassy conditions or light NE berg winds. Can't handle strong wind, but handles light westerly, or even SW or S, as long as it's light.

CAPE ST MARTIN ★★★ ⬛ 👑 ⬛

Fun little left-hander on a kelpy reef. Works on a southerly or SE wind. Picks up more swell than Heaven or Pastures. Requires similar swell size as Elands Bay.

TREKOSKRAAL ★★ ⬛ ⬜ 👑 ⬛

Fun little camping spot with excellent crayfish diving. A small right-hander that rolls into a small deep bay. Needs specific deep groundswell conditions and light easterly or berg wind conditions. Not very consistent.

VREDENBERG POINT ★★★★ ⬛ 👑 ⬛

A left pointbreak. Needs high tides, a clean 4–8' swell and light glassy variable winds, or a NE berg wind. Deep water off the rocks make it slightly scary, but it gets classic. Some distance north of Saldanha Bay. It's the same shape as the Kom. The wedge focuses and pitches steeply. You have to paddle hard. Breaks in front of a boulder, or next to it. If you make the drop, you fly down a rearing wall.

ELANDS MAGIC...ELANDS MAGIC...ELANDS MAGIC...ELANDS

strange and untouchable as a Hindu goddess, and, we would whisper reverentially to each other, 'She smokes zol bru, I've checked her!'

By the time the Kombi hit the last dirt track stretch towards the cluster of simple houses and conspicuous green hotel that makes up the better part of the town at Elands Bay, it was approaching sunset. We were the mighty pioneers of the West, riding into town on our faithful steed as the villagers made way for our great envoy. Well, actually, it was more like our steed

was limping in at a pitiful pace with a mangled fan belt, and the old tannie at the local café sighed and rolled her eyes like she knew what was coming.

Nevertheless, the afternoon spent getting there had felt like days and by now we were well aware of our hardened traveler status. Running down to the point along the windy, desolate beach, the sight of endlessly peeling three foot lefts had our tiny mob transfixed – this wasn't some local beach-break. Oh no. This was the big time. After what surely rated as the best surf

However, it's usually out of control when the swell is more than 5'. It's powerful for its size. Good in small swell and glassy berg breezes. Doesn't like wind. Faster and more powerful than Elands Bay, but more fickle.

SWARTRIET *** ● �

You need to pay a small toll to enter the beach area. A peaking, fun beachbreak that works in 2–4' conditions and light SE–NE breezes or glassy conditions.

YZERFONTEIN **** ■ ⌂ 👑

Good option if you want to get away from Cape Town for a couple of hours. The break is sometimes referred to as Schaap Eiland. It's a crunchy wedge-shaped wave that breaks over a flat slab of rock, then links with sand bars on the beach. More often than not, a freight train close-out is the result, but occasionally this wave is insanely hollow, and could host a Cape Town tourist bus inside it. Needs glassy or berg wind conditions.

SILWERSTROOM **** ■ ⌂

When the swell is tiny on the peninsula and the ocean is glassy, surfers often get lucky at Silwerstroom (Silver Stream). A sandbar close to the beach produces right of left peaks, sometimes approaching excellent quality. Recently, the owner blocked access by road, and you have to walk quite far to get there, from the boom gate at the entrance.

KREEFTE REEF **** ■ ⌂

Bowling right-hander breaks on the outside when big. Medium swell and low tide.

IC...ELANDS MAGIC...ELANDS MAGIC...ELANDS MAGIC...ELAN

we'd all ever had up until then, we returned to our campsite to set up our tents.

Scrambling around in the cold darkness, it was soon decided that the tents could wait until after we had checked out the local night-life. This amounted to the sum total of the hotel bar, complete with two pool tables and walls covered in old *Springbok Magazine* and *Scope* posters. When you're all of fifteen, it doesn't take much to impress and this seemed like a pretty happening place to be. Ordering ciders in our deepest voices, we strutted

round the pool tables and reminisced about the day's exploits while predicting what the next morning would be like. Somewhere between the third cider and the second game of pool, or perhaps the other way around, things got blurry and we returned to the camp. The tents seemed a much harder task than before so we opted to sleep under and around the Kombi instead.

'Jaslyk, it sounds big ay, bru?!' Warren said again. He'd already walked to the point and back and the sun wasn't even up

VAN RIEBEEK ★★ ● ⬜ ▮

Fickle beachbreak in Melkbos (North of Ou Skip caravan park). Mushy but can be good fun. Best in light NE winds and small swell.

CAPTAINS ★★★ ■ ⬜ 👑 ▮

Fickle reef / sand breaks in Melkbos. Consistency depends on sandbanks and conditions. Best in light SE or NE. Doesn't like big swell. Best in 2–4' clean groundswell. Fun peaks.

BEACH ROAD ★★★★ ■ ⬜ ▮

A classic right-hand sandbar point at Melkbos. It is protected by an outer reef. Works in light SW or SE winds and a big groundswell. The outside is best in the low tide, while the inside cooks on the high tide.

HOLBAAI ★★★ ● ⬜ ▮

Between Haakgat and Melkbos. Little dust road and small dunes. Beachbreak peaks. Prefers light easterly winds. Swell can't be too big either.

HAAKGAT ★★★ ■ ⬜ 👑 ▮

Sectiony left point and beach breaks, inconsistent and exposed, depends on sandbank, boiling reef section at the left point. Needs a high tide. The break is 30 m out and parallel to the beach. A line of rocks stop at Haakgat. A-frame peaks at the back go right across the rocks, but are difficult to ride.

yet. I soon discovered that the ground we'd fallen blissfully asleep on the night before felt more like hard rubble without a Hunters Gold or two inside you, a real man's drink. I thought my eyes weren't opening properly, but then realised it was the thick morning mist that was blocking out the icy ocean, which breathed at regular intervals in deep rumbles of white-wash.

If we had thought the previous day was as good as it gets, well, then we must have gone straight on to heaven. The new swell was bigger and thicker, but by the time the midday offshore came through it was sculpting the raw slabs of Atlantic juice into well-groomed walls that funneled perfectly along the mussel-encrusted shelf. A barren mountain loomed like a lonely sentinel against the elements behind us, and in the distance the windswept beach stretched on up the African continent for as far as our imaginations would allow.

The fact that the weekend crowd from Cape Town arrived steadily throughout the day didn't seem to bother us. As far as we

One of many West Coast lefts.

Hollow beachbreak in Melkbos, p. 68.

DERDE STEEN **** ■ ⌂

A fun beachbreak about 25 minutes north of Cape Town. It can't handle a big swell, nor too much wind. At it's best in glassy 2–5' conditions, left and right peaks can provide lots of entertainment.

TWEEDE STEEN ** ■ ⌂

A similar beachbreak setup to Derde Steen, except a lot more fickle and lacking the same quality.

EERSTE STEEN *** ■ ⌂

Hollow peaking beachbreaks on the coast road past Melkbos.

HORSE TRAILS *** ■ ⌂

So named due to a nearby estate that used to belong to Terence Millard, a famous racehorse trainer. His house used to be the only one around, and used to boast a traffic light for grooms to take horses across the road. It is a hollow-peak beachbreak. Can be seen if you stand on top of your car at the road. Breaks slightly differently to Derde Steen. A–frames break in small swell up to 5'.

KAMER VAN 17 **** ■ ⌂

A left, sandy point. It's pretty sectiony. Works in SE winds or on a calm day. Best on the low tide in a moderate swell. The spot is situated on the other side of the outcrop of rocks at the end of Big Bay.

were concerned, this was the cutting edge of surf adventure. We surfed the impossibly long jelly-legged lefts all day, often getting beaten but occasionally catching a smoker or two. Eventually it was time-out, and the sun that had blazed a trail across the stark west coast sky dipped languidly behind the crayfish factory that jutted out at the point where the headland met the sea. Back at the camp, a feeble effort was once again made to assemble the tents, but the stony ground refused to yield to our tent pegs.

Someone ingeniously thought that a bunch of rocks would do fine to hold the tents sturdy, and it was at about then that my sister's friend offered us one of her zol cigarettes. We all tried to act cool, like exotic babes offered us illegal narcotics all the time, but blew it when each of us hacked and coughed in succession on the anorexic spliff.

Convinced of our status as real men of the world after that, we strode into the hotel bar with an extra swagger in our steps. Being a Saturday evening, it seemed

BIG BAY ★★★ ■ ⊂⊐ ▥

A windy beachbreak popular with sailboarders. Big, A-frames break on the outside, then re-form before hitting the shorebreak. Sometimes there are good banks here, but it gets very crowded. Best in berg winds, or calm conditions. Can be disorganised and messy. Big Bay is one of the few West Coast spots that can cope with a NW wind, up to around 15 knots.

LITTLE BAY ★★ ● ⊂⊐ ▥

Marginal beachbreak. Enough said. Hangout for rats of the human kind. A few dribbly little peaks sometime.

TABLEVIEW ★★★ ■ ⊂⊐ ▥

In front of the old Doodles Restaurant. Similar to Blouberg (Big Bay). Deep outer sand bars break in bigger swell, while the shorebreak sand banks break on the re-form or stand-alone waves when it's smaller. Can't cope with too much wind. Crowded, but lots of peaks available, varying in quality and length of ride. Difficult to get really good waves, due to an irregular re-form that sometimes waits for the shorebreak before it decides to break.

SUNSET BEACH ★★★ ■ ⊂⊐ ▥

Scattered beachbreaks at a relatively new suburb called Sunset. Can get quite good in light NE winds and a solid 8' ocean groundswell, which translates to shifty 4–5' peaks, with a long walling right when at its best. This stretch of coast north of Cape Town is well known for being fickle, and only works in NE bergwinds.

IC...ELANDS MAGIC...ELANDS MAGIC...ELANDS MAGIC...ELAN

that every farmer in a 100 km radius had converged on the bar. We ordered beers this time in our gruffest voices, battling to be heard against the sakkie music pumping out of the huge speakers in the background. Everything was going just fine until Beaver, a more paranoid member of our crew, told the proprietor's wife his real age. For some reason this woman had been talking to him at the bar and he naturally assumed that if she was talking to him, she must be coming onto him. When she asked him his age, he thought that here was an older chick who digs younger guys. In his mind, by telling her the truth, he was going to get lucky.

When she heard he was all of sixteen, it was over. She disappeared and shortly after a very staunch, salt-of-the-earth type with watermelon forearms approached Beaver and told him in no uncertain terms that his underage patronage was not appreciated, nor any else of our crew. A few of us pretended we didn't know him, nonchalantly avoiding eye contact, and stayed on to shoot pool while they hastily made a

The closer to the city, the smaller the swell because the swell window begins to disappear, with the coast blocked by the northern corner of the Cape Peninsula. This is the case at Milnerton, where a long stretch of empty beach has a few waves. Best when a huge groundswell is runing on the other side, and it's glassy or light to moderate southeasterly.

DUMPS ★★ ■ ⌂

A fickle wave that gets quite good on occasion. It's at the mouth of the lagoon. Best on a high tide and a big, clean westerly groundswell and light berg winds. Not the kind of wave that is actively sought out.

THE WEDGE ★★★ ■ ⌂

Tucked away in the corner near Cape Town harbour, The Wedge is the first surf spot on the stretch of beach that runs all the way to Blouberg. You have to park in the harbour and clamber over concrete 'dollose' to access this spot. The swell does weird and wonderful things here. As it refracts round the harbour wall, it bounces and travels sideways to join another swell in a sharp triangular peak that can be very hollow at times. However, the take-off is often the best part of the wave, because it devotes most of its energy to the initial barrel. Best in any east wind. Needs a huge general swell to filter all the way around to the Wedge.

bee-line for the camp. Eventually we too left the bar in a squeamish haze of retreat. Some farmer had completely freaked us out by giving his Rottweiler a hand-job at the bar, much to the amusement of his drinking buddies.

So, with things getting more surreal than a David Lynch double-matinee, a little sleep seemed like a very good option. At first we thought we were at the wrong campsite when we couldn't find any of our tents, but then saw the unmistakable silhouette of the old Kombi, minus our tents that were there earlier. The others were all sleeping on the ground again, and after some kicking and probing we discovered that the 'rocks instead of tent pegs idea' hadn't been such a good idea after all. Most of our tents were well on their way to Angola, compliments of the Elands Southeaster, and so another night was spent sleeping on our gravel mattresses.

There reaches a point in every adventure, every journey, where the high swings to the low and effort outweighs reward. Sometimes it takes weeks, even months, to

Melkbos beachbreak. See p. 68.

HIC...ELANDS MAGIC...ELANDS MAGIC...ELANDS MAGIC...ELAN

reach this point. It took us all of two days.

By the time the old Kombi limped back onto the dirt roads homeward bound, pandemonium had broken loose.

Random bickering broke out about who had snored the loudest, or who had given who's board a Chinese wax job, and who was going to get dropped off first when we got back to Cape Town.

To make matters worse, we couldn't stop the car to pee because the stocking that was serving as a fan belt would come off, so anyone who had to go had to lean strategically out of the window, which wouldn't have been so bad, had my sister not done it.

To this day, someone still occasionally says to me in a disbelieving tone, 'Ay, remember that time when we were lightees, and your sister stuck her butt out the window on the way back from Elands? Jas bru, never seen anything like it ...'

CAPE PENINSULA

The Cape Peninsula hosts one of the most beautiful cities in the world. Cape Town, the capital of the Western Cape, lies on the north side and offers the most highly concentrated number of surf spots in South Africa. Cape Town is various things: the Fairest Cape, Tavern of the Seas, the Mother City and the Cape of Storms. Sir Francis Drake was astounded at the beauty of the Cape when he rounded Cape Point in the 16th century.

In the shadow of Table Mountain sprawls this city of three million people. It stretches into the distance across the Cape Flats. The old and the new mix to form a kaleidoscopic melting pot of cultures: from the Bokaap, home to the Muslim community; past the plush upmarket suburbs of Bantry Bay, Clifton, Constantia and Bishopscourt; and out to the sprawling townships of Gugulethu, Khayelitsha and Langa. Apart from the landmark flat mountain, which sports a tablecloth of cloud

Sean Holmes, Dungeons.

during the summer months when the Southeaster blows, the mountains form a backbone right down the peninsula, which is about 80 km long. For surfers, it's a dream come true, cold water notwithstanding. Cape Town is within an hour's drive of about 50 breaks, from bone-crunching reefs and hollow beachbreaks, to mellow sloping sand banks.

The largest concentration of breaks is on the west side of the Peninsula facing the Atlantic Ocean. The remainder line the eastern coastline, which faces the Indian Ocean. The following list includes most of the breaks on the peninsula from the harbour wall to the north, down the Atlantic side, around Cape Point (about 65 km from the city), up the east side to the seaside resort of Muizenberg and past, along the 40 km beach that stretches all the way from Muizenberg to Gordon's Bay.

THERMOPYLAE ★★★★ ■ 👑

A rare pointbreak in Cape Town, this wave breaks off the sunken remains of the wreck of a ship called the *Thermopylae* in Mouille Point. It's a left-hander that can produce really long walls as the wave travels along a rock shelf not far from the entrance to Cape Town harbour. The take-off zone can be a bit hairy, depending on the size of the swell and the tide. Because it faces north, and prevailing swell direction is south, an ocean swell of 10'+ is needed before this spot begins to break, unless the swell is westerly or northwesterly, which is fairly rare. There can be long lulls, unless a really big swell is running. An E-coli zone due to nearby sewage outlets.

OFF THE WALL ★★★★ ◆ 👑

The take-off zone of this city reefbreak is about the size of a Mini, yet up to 15 surfers, or more, can pack into it, waiting for a short, sharp take-off and long green wall that closes out at the end. Breaking along the promenade of a suburb called Mouille Point, adjacent to Sea Point, Off The Wall has vague similarities with its counterpart in Hawaii. The take-off is next to a retaining wall. Gets awesome.

ROCKLANDS ★★★ ◆ 👑

A gnarly left reef, down from Off the Wall, in Sea Point. It's best in SE winds, a large southwesterly swell and a pushing high tide. Can be working when the other Sea Point breaks are struggling to break. It wraps around the rocks and freight trains onto a rocky ledge, where it stands up and says, 'smack me or you die'. Experienced surfers only.

SOLLY'S ★★★ ■ 👑

A short reefbreak, breaking left and right, with an outer reef that works when big, depending on swell direction. Solly's is best in a clean 4–5' swell and light to moderate southeasterly winds. The spot is near the Pavilion, where all the Sea Point buzz is centered. A parking lot provides easy access. The outer reef gets really good sometimes.

QUEENS ★★★ ◆ 👑

Somewhat knobbly Sea Point left-hand reef. The take-off can get hairy. The swell concentrates on a ledging patch of rocks, then swings outwards. Can be big and mushy and fun. Needs a clean, solid 5–8' swell, high tide and SE winds or glassy conditions. While the northern Sea Point spots can handle a SW wind, Queens starts getting wobbly. The ride is not that long and, while quite consistent, does not get really good very often. Take care you don't ride into the rocks at the end.

GLEN BEACH ***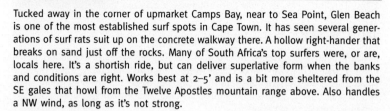

Tucked away in the corner of upmarket Camps Bay, near to Sea Point, Glen Beach is one of the most established surf spots in Cape Town. It has seen several generations of surf rats suit up on the concrete walkway there. A hollow right-hander that breaks on sand just off the rocks. Many of South Africa's top surfers were, or are, locals here. It's a shortish ride, but can deliver superlative form when the banks and conditions are right. Works best at 2–5' and is a bit more sheltered from the SE gales that howl from the Twelve Apostles mountain range above. Also handles a NW wind, as long as it's not strong.

LLANDUDNO ****

Another popular spot. Depending on the shifting sand banks, Llandudno can deliver awesome barrels. The 'Gat' is a thick wedge that breaks near the boulders to the right of the bay. The 'Gat' means 'Hole' in Afrikaans. It's a hard-breaking spitting tube. If the 'Gat' isn't working, there is usually a sand bar closer to the middle of the bay where a hollow right-hander breaks. Lefts can be ridden on the left side of the bay. It's often crowded and the water in summer is often freezing, down to 11°C after a particularly heavy upwelling, caused by galeforce offshore Southeasters that blow for days, pulling deep water to the surface. However, it's great thawing out in the hot sun afterwards! Can be a bit inconsistent. The sandbanks only deliver superlative waves at certain times of the year, mostly between spring and autumn. In winter, it tends to be out of control.

SECTIONS ***

A local called Mac lives near this spot – a small right-hander that peels past a granite boulder and into a small bay. Sometimes called Mac's Spot. You won't find it.

SANDY BAY ***

When Llandudno is closing out, Sandy Bay is a good option. This nudist colony is tucked away in the next bay and is a 20-minute walk from the car park. Mostly a short shorebreak wave, Sandy's can throw up perfect barrels on the shallow sand banks. It handles the Southeaster well and can cope with a southerly if not too strong.

DUNGEONS ****

One of a number of big wave spots ridden by a handful of Cape Town's hardcore crew. It has become part of the international big wave circuit, and is easily on a par with Mavericks or Todos Santos. Some say it's even better, because on the low tide it walls up like a giant freight train. Found just off the Sentinel mountain in

Hout Bay, this right-hander only starts breaking at about 10'. Best in light NW or glassy conditions. Needs a low tide, otherwise it gets too 'thick' (too much water).

HOUT BAY ★ ● ⌐⌐

In this fishing village, tucked around from the Sentinel, waves can be found off the harbour wall and down the beach. However, the swell window is small and the spots need a big swell to push into Hout Bay. The waves are generally short, small and of poor quality, although on a huge SW swell and NW winds, the harbour wall has been known to get good.

THE HOEK ★★★★★ ◆ ⌐⌐

The wedging perfection of the Hoek could inspire one to poetry. It's round. It's freezing cold. It's green. The descriptive phrase for a barrel, the 'Green Room', could have been coined here. Potent wedging A-Frame barrels break on a shallow sand-bar in crisp, clean water and a majestic setting. An offshore reef seems to concentrate the swell on to the sand bar at the Hoek, below spectacular Chapman's Peak Drive. When at it's best, this wave is a world class tube, short but round and perfect. Often one has to tuck in on take-off, due to a lip that throws fast and hard. Protected, slightly, from the Southeaster (offshore here), The Hoek works on a low tide and copes, just, with swell at 6–7', although you have to be selective.

NOORDHOEK BEACH ★★★★ ■ ⌐⌐

A beautiful beach that runs from Chapman's Peak Drive to Kommetjie. It's punctu-ated by a series of sand banks that deliver waves of various lengths, shapes and sizes. Some peaks get close to perfect along the beach, depending on sand move-ment and swell quality. Southeast winds are offshore. Occasionally a sand bank will form that delivers perfect waves, otherwise most peaks are fun.

DUNES ★★★★★ ◆ ⌐⌐

The Dunes was even better years ago. The sand that blew off high dunes into the sea does not move as much after alien vegetation took over. However, it must have been a vision from God in those days, because today it still delivers awesome barrels. On a solid 6–8' day, this spot delivers barrel after spitting barrel. Howev-er, be warned, it might look perfect from the beach, but be prepared for a over-worked pituitary gland. A wipeout can rip your booties off, snap your board and break your bones. For experienced surfers only, and those prepared for a mega-walk along the beach.

Cape Fur Seals.

Seals and Otters

When surfing in the southern Cape, in Cape Town or along the West Coast, you might encounter playful seals, and even otters. There are millions of Cape Fur seals in the Atlantic. Seal Island, near the infamous Dungeons break – South Africa's answer to the big wave spot of Mavericks – is covered with seals. When surfing in the Cape, you might even spy a Cape Clawless Otter in the lineup near you, hands to mouth, nibbling on some frshly caught prey. These mammals are totally comfortable in seawater, using powerful hind legs to attack their prey and human-like hands to hold their meal while feeding.

Whales

The main species of whales off the coast of South Africa is the Southern Right Whale. The breeding season is between July and October, when they come right into the bays of the Cape Pensinsula and the southern Cape. Hermanus and parts of False Bay are world-famous whale watching spots.

Penguins

The species of penguin found along the coast is known as the Jackass or African Penguin. The Jackass Penguin gets its name from the donkey-like braying call of the males. Normally found on small islands in the Atlantic and Indian Oceans, a breeding colony has established itself at Boulders Beach near Cape Town. Tourists can come close to the penguins. There is also a large colony of penguins on Robben Island.

Perlemoen (Abalone)

These valuable shellfish are generally found in the southwestern Cape from Agulhas to the Cape Peninsula and up the West Coast to Saldanha Bay. Prized by the eastern countries, perlemoen are poached remorselessly. They are good eating, but only if prepared correctly. You may not collect them between 1 August and 31 October, and the daily limit is four per person. The shell must be at least 11,43 cm across. Perlemoen must be swiftly prised off the rock before they clamp down with powerful sucker pads.

KAKAPO ★★ ■ ⌂

Just down from Dunes, there is an old wreck embedded in the sand. Only the boiler of the Kakapo sticks out, and occasionally the ribbed remains of the hull. Near it there is a shorebreak that provides crunchy barrels. Fickle and closes out a lot.

SUNSET ★★★★ ◆ ⌂

Just beyond Dunes, out to sea, lies a bombora. It's a big-wave oasis in the middle of the ocean. The swell must be 8' or more before it begins to break. The crew who surf Dungeons will go out here on those fun 20' days. Sunset, similar to its namesake in the Pacific Ocean, is a huge peak that features those jaw-dropping take-offs that seem to go on forever. A giant shoulder follows briefly before this grand daddy is laid to rest in a deep channel. Mostly a take-off. Doesn't offer the giant walls of Dungeons. Surfers are dropped off by rubber duck. Some are towed into the waves, only letting go once they are riding the shoulder of the wave.

KRANS OR KRONS ★★★ ■ ⌂

A shorebreak wave just to the right of Long Beach. It's popular among bodyboarders due to the sucking barrel. Very fast and hollow. Often dumps a long closeout section on to a boiling sandbar.

LONG BEACH ★★★★ ■ ⌂

Another established Cape Town surf spot peopled by masses of up and coming surf rats. Tucked away behind a point at Kommetjie, it's one of few places that can handle a southwesterly wind. Because it's so far around the corner – it actually faces North – the waves have to bend all the way around, almost doing a U-turn. The result, though, is a clean left-hand peak. The peaks break on the outside and run for about 20–40 metres before finishing off in a shorebreak closeout. A very rideable wave that's perfect for testing maneouvers. A lot of contests are held here.

BONEYARDS ★★★ ■ ⌂

Travelling around from Long Beach brings you to a series of outer reefs. Boneyards is an outer reef where long walling waves break over kelp beds. Best when it's glassy and a westerly groundswell is running. It entails a long paddle, but can be an insane wave when perfect. Inconsistent.

INNER KOM ★★ ● ⌂

On the inside section at Outer Kom, there is a miniature point. You have to sit virtually in the kelp. Waves that have bent around from the Outer Kom, travelled through the kelp and re-formed close to the rocks have all but lost their energy, but provide fun walling little lefts up to about 3'. Lots of youngsters hang out along the rocks here, honing their skills for the day they paddle out at the Kom.

OUTER KOM ***** ♦ ⚊

Another landmark wave in Cape Town. The Kom is a point / reef, where peaks break powerfully on the outside of a small point. Don't get caught inside. You'll suffer the ignominy of defeat, and the shifting peaks will ensure you only reappear where you started from. The Kom is at its best in a big, clean, westerly groundswell and glassy offshore conditions. It can handle a mild northwester, and turns on in NE offshore berg winds. Can handle a light SE and even a light S.

THE BOILER *** ♦ ⚊

Just to the left of the Kom, in front of the lighthouse, is a juicy right-hander. It isn't ridden very much, and only works at about 4–6' in certain conditions. A fairly short ride, it can be fun, as long as the waves are not closing out. This is because the break is sandwiched between a series of reefs. When it's too big, the waves break further out and it's not viable.

365 ***** ♦ ⚊

There are two theories to how it got its name – because the wedging barrel is so round it's 360 degrees plus another 5, or because there is a wave here 365 days of the year. It appears that the first is correct. Further down from the Kom, 365 is a classic but fickle outside reef that can produce epic waves. You usually can't surf it on the low tide for two reasons: the kelp on the way out is a nightmare to negotiate, and the rocky ledge on which it breaks gets too shallow, making for heart-stopping double-up ledges. However, when a very clean westerly swell is running, it can be surfed in any tide, and can cook on the low tide, when the inside reef becomes a top-to-bottom tube. This wave gets world class, and has been likened to Backdoor Pipeline when at its best. Needs glassy, or light north-westerly, conditions and a clean 5–8' groundswell. Gets perfect in a westerly swell and NE breeze.

I&J'S *** ■ ⚊

There are a number of rideable spots to the left of 365. A couple are re-formed waves that break on inside reefs, and a right-hander further down that allegedly gets pretty good. These waves are rarely surfed because few people have bothered exploring the area. A couple of locals swear by the quality of the right-hander, and the re-form looks like fun. The gnarly left that breaks towards 365 on the other side of the channel is sometimes called, you guessed it, 364.

CRAYFISH FACTORY ★★★★★ ◆

The most commonly ridden big wave spot in Cape Town. Named because it breaks just off a reef at a crayfish factory, this is probably Cape Town's scariest wave next to Dungeons. This regal right-hander only breaks when it deems fit to grace us with its power. Often when the swell is going off all over the peninsula, and The Kom is cranking at 6', the Factory has no waves at all. But when the groundswell begins hitting the 10' category and is coming from the southwest, the awesome Factory turns on. The swell hits a ledge and does things that will make your skin crawl. A walling, sucking, spitting monster made of glass, heaves its innards all over the kelp. Don't get caught inside. Several near-death experiences have occurred here. In fact, just about everyone who has surfed here will recount a tale of terror. The most common is wiping out on take-off, being pounded into the kelp and being held down for eons as 12 footer after 12 footer smash on to the ledge. When you surface, you'll be floating in the channel way down the reef after a lengthy underwater tour.

WITSANDS ★★ ●

This spot is everything the Crayfish Factory isn't, even though it's only a few hundred metres away. Featuring boring and shifty sand-bottomed peaks, with rips and channels all over the place, Witsands is the last resort if your surf mission has failed to deliver. However, even when it's cooking you might land up at Witsands, albeit via a different medium. It's your likely destination if you have fall victim to the Factory's habit of sending you packing in a rip that tears across the bay in a huge swell. Witsands includes Barclays Bank, a sandbank that cooks occasionally.

MISTY CLIFFS ★★ ■

Further down, is·a misty beach aptly named. Believe it or not, it has also been the destination for poor souls spat out of the back end of the Factory. It's a fickle sand-bar – mostly rights – that only works when the swell is clean, usually when other spots are too small.

SCARBOROUGH BEACH ★★★ ●

There are three possible breaks here: a small right-hander that peels along a rip channel in the left corner, a peak in the middle of the beach and a right-hander off rocks in front of the car park. A clean westerly swell and light offshores turn on the car park although the beach is more consistent. Re-forming right-handers, having wrapped around an outside point, swing back into the beach and break on a sand-bar alongside a deeper channel along the rocks of the inside point. The rip keeps the sand out and on the sandbar. Gets perfect here, but a little inconsistent. For its size, it's pretty juicy. Best at 2–4'.

Dias Beach, p. 85.

SCARBOROUGH POINT ★★★ ■

This fickle left-hand point needs the right conditions to work. A westerly swell is the first requirement. A light easterly is the second. A pushing tide is the third. These three don't occur simultaneously all that often, but when they do, it's the closest wave on the Atlantic side to an actual pointbreak, apart from Thermos.

OLIFANTS BOS ★★★★ ■

There are a number of waves in the Cape Point Nature Reserve that have some good surf. The surf spots here used to be secret until the late 1990s. However, they get pretty crowded these days, despite the expensive car and board fees at the gate. Rocky right pointbreak which works on southeast winds and moderate to large west to southwest swell. Best on the incoming tide.

PLATBOOM ★★★★ ◆

It breaks a bit in the kelp, but produces some excellent waves. It screams down a rocky ledge, going left. At its best in a light berg wind or moderate NW winds and a large, clean 6–8' westerly groundswell. Works when the Factory does, but the swell shouldn't be too huge.

EXTENSIONS ★★★★ ■ ▭

Extensions gets hollow and fast. A rocketing right-hander that's a bit mushy in every-day conditions, the wave flies down a rock shelf and sandbank combined, then refracts around a corner into a channel. When good, you can take-off over towards the middle of the beach, extracting more juice out of a barrelling take-off zone. Best in easterly winds, or a light to moderate northwesterly.

TO TAKE OFF AND LIVE AT DUNGEONS

By Steve Pike

Less than a kilometre from a Hout Bay quayside where tourists dine on fresh seafood, the thunder of big surf can be heard at the Sentinel, Cape Town's famous landmark. These are not ordinary waves. As the white water recedes into the Atlantic Ocean, another wave rears up. It smothers the horizon, and a portion of the sky. Measuring three to four storeys, it does not look friendly. This is Dungeons, the meanest surf spot in Africa. South

Africa's top big wave surfers pursue the ultimate adrenaline rush here.

The big event of the year is Red Bull Big Wave Africa. If the three week waiting period, starting at the end of May, does not yield waves reaching at least 18', it's held over until the next year. According to big wave rider Cass Collier, Dungeons is one of the most dangerous waves on earth, and he has surfed many of the biggest.

'It's not like the big waves at Waimea

UNDERWATER POINT ★★★ ◆ ⌂

This right-hander works off another rocky reef. Offers an insane barrel at times. Watch out for the rocks about halfway down which shorten the ride. If it wasn't for this closeout section, the wave would carry on for another 30 metres or so.

DIAS BEACH ★★★ ■ ⌂

Bodyboarders still speak in awe of the day Mike Stewart was taken here and blew the place apart. It was never regarded as a surf spot until recently. Just around the corner from the sheer cliffs of Cape Point, it's an imposing venue. It also entails a stiff walk down and a steep half-hour climb back up. There is not much beach, just rock, cliffs and a crunchy right-hander that breaks close to the rocks. Better suited for bodyboarders, it has been ridden by standups too.

....FALSE BAY

BUFFELS BAY ★★★★ ◆ ⌂

A classic right-hand pointbreak tucked away in the Reserve, on the False Bay side. Befriend a local if you want to surf it. It is fiercely protected. Needs an enormous swell – a 15–20' southerly swell – to push into the swell window that protects False Bay from the brunt of the ocean. When it's working, the veterans venture from the woodwork, or should that be a woodie panel van? It's a difficult wave to master because it holds off in deep water, then suddenly jacks up on the outside of this point and races down the rocks into a small bay. Buffels only starts working at about 6', and can be inconsistent unless the swell is coming from a mega cyclonic system out to sea. But once you've caught a wave, you get a classic walling wave that runs for a good 200 metres.

(Hawaii), Todos Santos (Mexico) or even Mavericks (California). It's colder. It's more powerful in the sense that it's not a huge peak that fades. It's a huge walling pointbreak. You are committed to riding it. If you fall off, you pay the price.' That price of course can mean death.

Hawaiian surfer Mark Foo once told a journalist: 'I'm not afraid of dying ... if you want the ultimate thrill, you've got to be willing to pay the ultimate price. To me it's not tragic to die doing something you love.'

Foo died several years ago while surfing 20' Mavericks in California.

One of the KwaZulu-Natal contingent – John Whittle, 32, a devout Christian, sailor and former Springbok surf lifesaver – is known for his fearless approach. 'Dying is no major sweat,' he said during the waiting period of the inaugural Red Bull event in 1999. Turns out the swell didn't reach the right size and the event was held over until 2000, when it reached 18' on the last day.

'Sure,' says Whittle, 'I don't want to die.

BLACK ROCKS **** ◆

This spot is more consistent, but also needs a huge ocean swell to push into the swell window between Cape Point and Hangklip. Remains jealously guarded, even though it gets radically overcrowded, with a bunfight in the small take-off zone. If you don't know the spot, or the guys in the water, don't expect waves. A peak breaks on a rock shelf and runs both ways. The right is the more powerful wave. It's a classic wedge setup and handles up to close on 10' in ideal conditions (westerly winds and clean groundswell). For it to be this big though, you need a massive SE swell in the 15–20' category. Although False Bay has a fairly big swell window, it faces more east than south. Most swell comes from the S or SW. It is inconsistent and usually has long lulls between sets.

FISH HOEK * ●

This is basically a large retirement home. It's a sleepy town on the False Bay coast. The waves that break along its pretty beach are generally this way too. In the left-hand corner – Clovelly Corner – some small waves are ridden by clans of grommets.

GLENCAIRN ** ■

Two little breaks at this small suburb between Kalk Bay and Fish Hoek: a short, hollow left reef and a weak little beachbreak on a par with Fish Hoek. The reef likes glassy conditions, and a clean 3–4' groundswell pushing into False Bay. It's a low tide wave. Bodyboard-friendly.

But the fear of dying is not really part of me when surfing.'

He conceded that when paddling for a huge wave 'your adrenalin pumps. Your heart beats faster. Thoughts rush through your mind. But death is not one of them. Your survival instinct overrules everything ... When I paddle for a big wave, I have no idea what will happen next. Then I make the wave, you know, survive it and I'm ready for the next one.'

However, if you don't make the wave at Dungeons, be prepared to hold your breath for a long time. The imposing venue is also intimidating. It's a storm-blasted collection of jagged rocks and reefs wedged between the cliffs of the Sentinel, the deep ocean and Seal Island, the popular tourist attraction. It loses this attraction when one considers that seals are the favourite food of the Great White shark.

However, Collier said that when it gets big, other factors were insignificant. 'It makes no difference if a wave is 15, 20 or 25'. After a certain size, it's big, and stays

The Hoek, p. 78.

Llandudno, p. 77.

KALK BAY REEF ★★★★★ ◆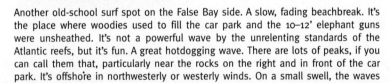

Another world-class reef wave, but intensely localised. Not that the locals are to blame. It's probably the take-off zone, which is the size of a manhole cover. When it's good, this insanely hollow left resembles Pipeline. Many a hottie has cut his barrel-riding teeth on this wave. There is a curious quirk here. When the South-easter blows, it's onshore everywhere else, but due to a contour effect from the mountains behind and above it, the wind is channeled offshore at the reef.

DANGER REEF ★★ ■ ⌃⌄

Dangers is a left and a right that breaks on a rocky ledge just down from Kalk Bay. It's a deceptively powerful wave that breaks off a small, shallow rock shelf, best just past the low tide. Best on a SE swell and a light NW wind. Gets intense, with a thick lip that sucks over a tight, bodyboard-friendly tube.

BAILEY'S REEF ★★★ ■ ⌃⌄

This is usually a short right-hand reefbreak in front of Bailey's Cottage, a historical monument. It's best on a northwesterly wind, a clean 4–5' groundswell and a spring high tide. Can get pretty hollow.

MUIZENBERG (CORNER) ★★ ● ⌷

Another old-school surf spot on the False Bay side. A slow, fading beachbreak. It's the place where woodies used to fill the car park and the 10–12' elephant guns were unsheathed. It's not a powerful wave by the unrelenting standards of the Atlantic reefs, but it's fun. A great hotdogging wave. There are lots of peaks, if you can call them that, particularly near the rocks on the right and in front of the car park. It's offshore in northwesterly or westerly winds. On a small swell, the waves

big.' Dungeons offers the right ingredients for adrenalin-charged extreme sports – awesome power, terror, sharks, deep ocean, kelp, cold water and a rugged but majestic setting. However, because of the distance between the waves and the land, it is not ideal for spectators, judges or surfers, who must rely on a boat to access the waves.

Former Springbok surfer Ross Lindsay said Dungeon's notoriety stemmed from the way each swell appeared suddenly from the deep ocean and hit a rock shelf.

With nowhere to go but up, each swell becomes a giant watery ledge. This was the moment to 'take off' or 'get sucked over the falls', meaning a 30' freefall and double impact with the sea and tons of collapsing water. It could also result in an underwater tour of the reef lasting several minutes.

A specific fitness is required. Big wave surfers need powerful lungs and the upper body strength to protect the lungs from bone-jarring impacts.

'You need all your air when held under for a few minutes,' said Lindsay, who break close to shore. When it's bigger, the outside breaks first and the wave re-forms again on the inside. Malibu boards are just right here because they give you enough momentum to make it all the way through. Alternatively, you can pump your 6' 2" up and down like a jack-in-the-box on acid to impress your girlfriend.

CEMETERY ★★★

Similar setup to Muizenberg, but with more juice. Also westerly winds, and a few peaks to choose from, lefts and rights. Expect the swell to be at least one to two foot bigger, and slightly hollower.

NINE MILE REEF ★★★

Further down False Bay towards Gordon's Bay is Nine Mile Reef. It's only a reef in as much as the sand has collected around rocks. The wave breaks on a sand bank. Lefts and rights can be enjoyed here.

MONWABISI - STRAND ★★

Lots of sandbanks along this stretch, with lots of potential, and a few secret spots. Near Monwabisi are sandstone cliffs and a beach entertainment complex. It often looks bigger than the other spots in False Bay, but few take the trouble to explore.

STRAND ★★★

There are several sand and rock bottomed breaks in the area. Most popular is the Pipe, which gets pretty good. It's offshore in NE-SE winds. The further around to Muizenberg you go, the more offshore the N-NW becomes. According to the locals, this place has good waves.

ONS...TO TAKE OFF AND LIVE AT DUNGEONS...TO TAKE OFF AND LIVE

assisted in the formation of the High Performance Laboratory, part of the Sports Science Institute in Cape Town, that aims to optimise surfing performance.

Despite much inactivity, big wave surfers had to stay in good shape. 'When a swell arrives, you must be ready to put your body on the line at short notice.'

According to Micky Duffus, big wave charger and former contest director, veteran Cape waterman Pierre de Villiers pioneered Dungeons, but, true to his roots, declined to compete. He believed

there was an ethical schism between the act of surfing and act of competing. 'Pierre commands the most respect. He is the true reflection of what big wave surfing is all about.'

Despite their differences, according to Lindsay, South African big wave riders are kinsmen 'bonded by a love for big wave surfing'.

How do they maintain this affinity when facing situations terrifying to most people? Collier believes that commitment is the key. Lindsay agrees, 'Absolute faith and

When a massive storm swell is breaking, a big left-hander just off the harbour wall begins to break. The ride ends at Bikini Beach. It gets perfect, and used to be ridden by a handful of stoked locals. However, the mystique is gone and almost everyone who owns a board knows about this place. Some days there are 30 guys out. Lately, according to locals, the spot has been getting wrong swell directions, and the waves have been closing out right across the harbour. However, with the right southeasterly push and a light northerly wind, or a southeaster in the wake of a 12–18' swell from a big cold front, it goes off. Loses a star for inconsistency.

TO TAKE OFF AND LIVE AT DUNGEONS...TO TAKE OFF AND LIVE AT DU

commitment. Fitness is important, but equipment is vital. One needs to take great care of your boards. If you have faith riding a board, you feel secure taking off on a big wave.'

Big wave surfboards are 8–10' long and unlike the heavy wooden Olos of ancient Hawaii, the modern 'rhino chaser' or big wave 'gun', is light and sleek, with extra thickness for buoyancy and momentum.

'You need something special in terms of weight, size or thickness to make it down the wave,' Lindsay said.

And the feeling?

'Therapeutic,' says Collier. 'The bigger the wave, the further away I am from land', he says, with a wry smile.

Mark Foo, before his tragic death, said: 'People see the height, they see the volume of the water and they see all this movement, but what they can't feel is the power. You're tapped into it, you're feeling it through your feet, your toes and your ankles. It's the ultimate rush.'

Kalk Bay reef, p. 88.

Sunset over Table Bay.

The Boland and Southern Cape regions are known for their scenic beauty. Cool and wet in the winter, warm and dry in the summer, it's a paradise of a unique kind. Kelp, whales and dolphins add to a rich and varied sea life. The mountain ranges form a spine that sweeps upwards towards the Eastern Cape. With names like the Boland, Outeniqua, Swartberg, Underberg and Houwhoek, it has a richness in heritage, and vast botanical variety unlike any found on the planet, comprising a stunning array of fynbos species: protea, pincushion, restios, erica (heather). The

Outer Pool, Mossel Bay.

region is rugged, with hills and thickly wooded ravines that snake upwards into the mountains. Here you find leopards, baboons, lynx, porcupines, buck, tortoises, rock rabbits, mongooses, honey badgers and lots more.

During winter, countless waterfalls cascade downwards towards the sea and many inland lagoons. The river water is rich in minerals, and runs a translucent rust-red colour. The surf is best in N or NW winds and clean groundswell, particularly in autumn and spring. In winter, the swell often gets too big.

KOEËL BAY **** ■

Sometimes referred to as the Caves, Koeël Bay is a beachbreak in front of low sand-stone cliffs, around the corner from Gordon's Bay. It's close to the beach, and looks like a closeout from the road above. A fairly fickle sandbar that often closes out. However, on a low tide and proper sand arrangement (especially in summer), some classic wedging 3' barrels are there for the taking. When you're in boardshorts and you're slotting into a pristine 4' tube, life takes on a sunny glow.

PARANOIA **** ♦

Like the name suggests, it will be the feeling you get when surfing it in a 6–8' swell as you lurch perilously close to some sharp, nasty looking rocks. A beach with a left-hand point break. It breaks almost on the rocks, and needs very glassy, clean, evenly spaced lines to work. Beginners, stay away.

MOONLIGHT BAY, HANGKLIP ** ■

Right-hander in small, rocky bay. It works the same as Pringles. SE offshore wind. Usually a bit bigger than Pringles. It works when you least expect it.

BETTY'S BAY *** ■

A fun right-hand beachbreak created from bigger swells that refract around a kelpy outcrop of rocks and re-form on a sand bar at about 3–4'. It sometimes looks better than it is, but it gets pretty good if you don't mind weekend crowds. The bigger waves seem to miss the sand bar and close out across the bay. However, sometimes one of the bigger waves will hold up just enough to provide a really hollow inside section ending in a long shorebreak barrel.

PRINGLE BAY ** ●

Tucked around the corner near Hangklip, this beach gets a few small waves, but is not generally known as a good surf spot. However, the left-hand point on the one side of the beach, breaks occasionally. Likes a solid SW swell and a SE wind. Gets hollow every now and then, particularly in the aftermath of a strong front after the wind has switched to SE.

HAARDEBAAI **** ♦

A big-wave right-hand reefbreak. It likes a large westerly swell and light NW winds. Gets excellent, but its unforgiving and will not be treated lightly, so be warned.

KLEINMOND ★★★ ■ ⌐

A left breaks towards the car park at Kleinmond, just before Hermanus, but it's fickle and the rip can make paddling out tough, especially if the swell is oversized. The outgoing rip between the rocks and the wave is created by a deep channel, favourite area for fishermen. The rip kicks when the swell gets to about 5–6'. A light NW or N wind is best.

ONRUS ★★★★ ■ ⌐ ⋈

A fun wedgy, little right-hander that breaks into a rip channel along some rocks to the left of this sleepy little holiday village. Lefts can also be found towards the middle of the beach. Onrus is a variable peak. The right conditions are light north-westerly conditions and a 3–5' swell. There is also a nearby beachbreak, which is comparable to Sandy Bay. It can get excellent.

DE KELDERS ★★ ◆ ⌐

Almost at Gansbaai, which is where the British war ship HMS Birkenhead sank, is a small cluster of houses along a dusty road, metres from the sea. At the end of the road, right in the corner, near a large Strandloper midden and interesting caves, is a fun but fickle little beachbreak that hardly anyone surfs. It's fun though and some barrelly lefts and rights can be had. A hectic rip makes it a wave for the experienced only. Word has it that more waves can be found further down this long beach, which basically goes all the way to Hermanus.

GANSBAAI ★★★ ■ ⋈

A few breaks in the area. Best conditions are light SE-NE and a clean groundswell in the 6–8' range and bigger. Mostly reefs. You have to contend with thick kelp. Great exploration possibilities. Most of the breaks can be found on the eastern side of Gansbaai, along a rocky, kelpy stretch of coast. Good crayfish diving here too.

PEARLY BEACH ★★★ ■ ⌐ ⋈

Good waves occasionally. A right-hand reefbreak. Best in a NE-NW breeze and clean groundswell. Some good waves along the beach. Rip currents can be a problem.

CAPE INFANTA ★★ ■ ⌐ ⋈

Right point. Needs big southerly swell. Lacks form. The beachbreak gets good in summer during a moderate swell. Also needs light westerly winds or a NW breeze.

JONGENSFONTEIN **** ■

When you're headed to Stilbaai in the belief that it will be firing, 'Jongens' might appease you if you are wrong about Stilbaai. Jongens prefers a smallish 2-4' swell, and breaks cleanly onto a pointbreak-ish reef. NW winds must be light, or glassy.

DOLPHIN POINT **** ♦

A gnarly, ledging right-hand pointbreak with some seriously hollow sections. Needs a solid 10'+ groundswell before the swell wraps into the bay. Needs a westerly wind. Only good surfers need apply.

STILBAAI ***** ♦

Another solid, powerful pointbreak. Despite a fickle rip that often pushes you down the rocks, this is a powerful, grinding right-hander. Like the other points around here, it needs a big swell. An ocean swell of 12' translates to 4–6' here. Needs clean, glassy offshores to be at its best. Best on a low tide.

GOURITS MOUTH **** ■ ⌷

A right pointbreak. A little surfed spot (hard to find) that breaks on sand that has built up over the rocks. It works in large SW groundswells and moderate westerly winds.

STRUISBAAI **** ♦

There are two main breaks. A symmetrical outside reef and a right-hand point called Maclears. The reef breaks to the left and right. Very sharky area. Like many of the bays in this area, the point needs a huge SW swell before there is enough juice to wrap the swell into a North-facing bay. Otherwise, an Easterly swell is needed.

ARNISTON *** ■ ⌷

A beautiful little white-washed fishing village with four spots in the area. Ask a local to show you around. Best in light W or NW winds and clean southerly swell.

VLEESBAAI ***** ♦

Protected point that breaks very rarely, in similar vein to Bruce's Beauties in Cape St Francis. It turns on when a massive southeasterly swell is pushed in by an incoming tide or strong SE winds. The onshore SE wind blows frontal groundswell back into the bay. This break is not a great option. Firstly, it is fickle, and breaks rarely. Secondly, it is hard to find. Thirdly, big Great White sharks breed in the area.

Sea urchins.

Red bait

So named because the sea squirt – a squidgy orange creature that lives inside a lumpy, soft covering – is often prised open and used as bait. Otherwise known as tunicates or ascidians, Red Bait is the most prolific of these species. Although they stink when dead and decomposing, the soft and squidgy texture has cushioned many a surfer when wiping out on a rocky reef. Sea squirts are part of a large number of invertebrates that live under rocks and in crevices along the South African coast.

Plough snail (bullia digitalis)

This green-coloured sea snail crawls around at the edge of the tidal zone on beaches all around South Africa. It digs into the sand on the incoming tide and it stays there until the tide recedes,

avoiding being left 'high and dry' in the hot sun. A slimy 'foot' doubles as an underwater sail. In moving water, the snail turns upside down and extends its foot to catch the currents.

Sea urchins

These prickly creatures can cause a lot of unnecessary pain. They are a species of shellfish protected by long needles. Mostly confined to the East Coast, they are found wedged between rocks in shallow water around the inter-tidal zone. When paddling out at Eastern Cape spots, you have to be careful. It takes time to get all the spines out, and the wounds can become infected. A famous spot infested with sea urchins is Nahoon Reef. If you stray off the concrete pathway out to the break, you may regret it.

Tucked away around a corner, this is the Bruce's of the southern Cape. It's an awesome barrel, but it only breaks when a solid southeasterly swell pushes around the corner and on to the rocks, in similar fashion to Vlees. Lots of sharks in the area. You don't really want to surf here.

...........MOSSEL BAY

Like Plettenberg Bay, Jeffrey's Bay and Port Elizabeth, Mossel Bay lies on the other side of a protruding point. In this case it's Cape St Blaize. Its southern shores are lined with awesome cliffs that loom above the thundering surf below. The rock strata is laid bare, and massive caverns have been cut out by the relentless force of the elements.

The town of Mossel Bay has grown considerably, mostly due to the massive Mossgas oil-from-gas project, where offshore gasfields are mined for gas that's converted to petroleum. Apart from the considerable number of staff that live in the area, Mossel Bay is essentially a holiday town. There are a number of surf spots in the town itself, along the northern coastline of Cape St Blaize.

Outer Pool is Mossel Bay's most famous wave. There are several backpackers spots, hotels and shops.

The area is steeped in history. Bartholomeu Dias, the Portuguese explorer who 'discovered' South Africa, landed for the first time at a place called Munro's Bay, a calm little cove 3 km around the corner from Cape St Blaize. There are numerous historic houses, including about 200 stone houses, built a century ago by Cornish stonemasons. In the distance, the jagged blue line of the Outeniqua Mountains maintain an eternal watch over the coast.

THOSE WERE THE DAYS...THOSE WERE THE DAYS...THOSE WERE THE D

THOSE WERE THE DAYS

By Byron Loker

One of the most ambitious surf trips we ever attempted was in the summer of 1992. We were one year out of school and the sweet freedom of drivers' licences, of-age IDs and Christmas holidays was ours to savour. Our plan was to head for Durban from Cape Town and surf everywhere in-between.

Our carriage was the Soltau family Peugeot, a silver beast that, strictly speaking, had no business driving to Durban, but

it's a good thing cars have no say in these matters.

My travelling companions were the brothers Soltau: Fred an aspirant lawyer, with a mane of tangled, curly blonde hair worthy of Samson or any hardcore surfer, and sure to afford us respect at any spot given to heavy localism. Chris, the strong silent one, with brooding good looks, sure to earn us attention of available young women, so we hoped, for surely such

INNER POOL ★★★ ■ 〜

Somewhat overrated, the Inner Pool is within a stones throw of Outer Pool. A small inlet where the waves break off rocks. Tends to be a bit slow moving and mushy, but is pretty popular. Walls up nicely sometimes, often when Outer Pool is flat.

OUTER POOL ★★★★ ◆ 〜

The main wave at Mossel Bay. Outer Pool gets big and hairy. This can mean a tough paddle against a rip that surges along the point and big walling waves that trick you into paddling too far on the inside. In a clean orderly swell and light westerly winds, this wave gets really good.

SANTOS REEF ★★ ■ 〜

Right in front of the caravan park at Mossels, Santos is a reef peak that needs a big swell and light SW winds. Gets quite good, although lacking raw power.

DING DANGS ★★★ ■ 〜

A fun wave that needs a huge swell to wrap around Cape St Blaize. Best in south-westerly winds. Needs a low tide.

DIAS BEACH ★★ ● ▭

Just past Mossel Bay, near where the road rejoins the highway, is a fickle beachbreak that depends on the sandbanks. Needs light offshore winds and a moderate swell.

attention was an integral part of any surf trip of this nature.

The swell was tiny in False Bay when we left. We skirted Koeël Bay and decided to take a look at Hawston, where we found a good 3-4' hollow wave. Got my first tube there, and as we drifted back past the shanty houses and cardboard shacks to which hardened fishermen returned, I considered myself lucky to have escaped from the harsh reality of life for those few hours we were in the water.

Mossel Bay was where the harsh reality of being on the road hit us. Actually it was more like a shot of Jack Daniels at 6 am that did us in. We arrived late in the afternoon in Mossels and there wasn't much swell about, so we pulled into the campground and got settled for our first night in the wild. Things all went a little awry from there. First, I tripped over a speed bump and lopped the end of my big toe off in an injury that required minor surgery when we eventually reached Durban. Next, Fred reversed the car into a tree and put a pretty serious buckle in the bumper. And

BRAK RIVER ★★★ ● ⬭

The long beach here gets lots of swell, although the surf is fickle. Again, light westerly winds are best, and it depends on the sandbanks. However, a good couple of secret spots deliver the goods for surfers who live in the holiday houses, along the top of a long, dune-based hill that runs parallel to the beach.

HEROLDS BAY ★★★★ ■ ⬭ 👑

Best in a clean groundswell with a slight Easterly or SE direction to it. It's a reefbreak and sandbar combined. Needs light N-NW bergwinds.

VIC BAY ★★★★ ■ 👑

Home of the southern Cape surfer, Victoria Bay is a classic setup on a small scale. Nestling between steep hills that run into the ocean, this bay is probably only 200 metres wide. The right side of the bay, an established holiday getaway for the fortunate few who have a house at the water's edge, is a point that produces perfect pointbreak walls. The takeoff is right near a rock that sticks out the water. It then walls away from you and down a shallow line of rocks. The bigger waves angle further away from the rocks and into the middle of the beach. Best at 2–6' and glassy or offshore conditions. Handles light to moderate southerly winds.

GERICKES POINT ★★★ ◆ 👑

To the West of Sedgefield, heading away from Knysna, lies a shale headland with a small left-hand pointbreak on the other side. It works in a small swell, and is one of few spots in the area that work in a NE onshore wind. It gets out-of-control very easily on account of the very small point setup. Doesn't like anything over 4'.

---

we hadn't even touched the stock in our amateur bar in the boot.

The only thing to do under the circumstances was to get started on that bar in the boot. The beers were finished pretty promptly, the sun had set and somehow the tent had erected itself. My toe was comfortably anesthetised, and Fred's imagination had been drawn from the punishment awaiting his mom's car's return. That left us with the matter of the bottle of Cane. It's accompanying bottle of Coke had long since been consumed and we were

stumped for a mixer, until Chris produced a can of Clifton. It was the most disgusting cocktail, but we soldiered on regardless, determined to push our adolescent freedom to the edges.

The rest of the evening was a bit of a blur. Memories drift in and out of focus like disjointed scenes of an unedited super8 movie projected onto a crumbling wall. In some scenes I can see us scaling a barbedwire fence and rolling down a steep, grassy bank. In another scene we arrived at this raging party. It looked like a cool place

Southern Cape beachbreak.

Provides fun and zippy hollow waves that break over volcanic rock. About a 20-minute walk from the car park. There is a big right-hander that crunches over a shallow reef just across from Gerickes. Looks mighty interesting, but dangerous.

GOUKAMMA RIVER MOUTH **** ■ ⌂

This wave can get epic when the sand is in the right place. The Goukamma River, with its deep, rich, red mineral colour from the forests and mountains of the southern Cape, trickles into the sea here. The ocean responds with superlative form. In light, northerly winds, this spot fires on all cylinders. About 20 km from the southern side of Knysna, at the mouth of the river, the peaks here can be superlative.

FISH BOMA *** ■ ⌂

Just off the carpark facing the Goukamma River is a peak that breaks on the other side of a rocky outcrop. It needs a lowish tide, a northerly or northeasterly breeze and 3-5' swell. Locals get some good waves here, although a shark attack in 2000 virtually stopped all activity here. As local Charles Smith reckons: 'I never thought our sharks would do this to us. It was quite a shock!'

BUFFALO BAY WILDSIDE *** ■ ⌂

The stretch of coast on the exposed side of Buffalo Bay. It gets messy easily and can't handle too much swell, because it comes directly on to the beach here, often breaking on outside banks and closing out. However, on smaller days when there is little wind or a breeze from the northeast, a clean and powerful left, breaks off a sand bank in the middle of the beach. Can get a bit rippy though. Occasionally, a wedge breaks in the corner on the right-hand-side of the beach. Locals say that its epic days have been over for some years, although there seems to be no reason why they shouldn't come back again.

when we got there, lots of nice people dancing and drinking and enjoying themselves. We felt right at home and took up seats at a beautifully decorated table festooned with delectable munchies. We tucked in heartily until this very nice lady in a hat with flowers on it, came over and introduced herself to us. She said she was delighted that we had come to celebrate her daughter's wedding, but that unfortunately we had not been catered for and would it be too much trouble if we were to leave? We obliged graciously. I fell down the stairs on the way out and stubbed my toe again.

We didn't surf the next day, there may have been surf, but I don't remember. Nevertheless before long we were on the road again, chasing, chasing. We arrived in East London and kept right on going, we had the smell of the 'Kei in our nostrils and wanted to get there soon so we could spend the rest of our days like Robinson Crusoe in the wild, surfing perfect blue pointbreaks and sampling the delights of the Kei's finest export.

BUFFALO BAY **** ■

A large bay near Knysna. There are a number of waves around Buffalo Bay. The point offers a fairly inconsistent right-hander that needs an easterly tinge to the swell for it to break properly. Generally, the usual southwesterly swells hit the outside point and wrap into the bay before re-forming and breaking on the inner point. This is the common B-Grade South African point setup. However, when the swell is coming out of the southeast or east, they instantly become A-grade spots. Similar setups include Coffee Bay, Bruce's Beauties and Seal Point. Buffalo Bay needs a westerly wind and anything from 3–8' swell.

BUFFALO BAY BEACH (MURPHYS) ** ■ ⌂

A fun left and right peak can be found quite far down the beach from the point at Buffalo Bay. Gets a rip that tends to pull you to the left, towards a churny and shallow reef / sandbank. However, some really fun and hollow inside waves, as well as the occasional solid left on the outside, can make this spot worthwhile. Best in a low to pushing tide and light westerly winds.

...........KNYSNA

Knysna lies on the north shore of the glistening Knysna lagoon. Surrounded by South Africa's largest tract of closed-canopy indigenous forest, Knysna lies in the midst of a natural paradise. The area is home to the brightly coloured Knysna Loerie bird, pansy shells, Dusky and Bottlenosed dolphins, Southern Right whales and South Africa's only forest elephants.

The town of Knysna lies on the 'Garden Route' – a 400 km stretch of coastline that is spectacularly beautiful. The town hosts flea-markets, craft shops and cosy cafés that ooze a rustic, small-town charm.

...THOSE WERE THE DAYS...THOSE WERE THE DAYS...THOSE WERE TH

We went off-road just outside East London, our Peugeot holding up magnificently over dongas and potholes the size of a cow. Eventually we reached Morgan's Bay, a place without a postcard, where we could begin to wean ourselves off civilization. We spent our days hiking along the beach and scouting for those secret surf spots we were determined to find. The aching solitude and desolate beauty of the place made us realised how much we, as a race, have lost in our endless quest for progress; for retail developments and time-share

franchises, highways and malls. After a few days at Morgan's Bay we drove onto the Kei River ferry. Armed with a bag of sweets to throw out to the kids that ran to the road, to wave us past, we headed for Umtata where we had to apply for a permit to camp at Coffee Bay. Here we encountered Third World bureaucracy. We spent hours wandering around deserted corridors, searching for non-existent offices in the Botha Sichau Building, before eventually securing our permit and making the trek back towards Coffee Bay.

The majestic Outeniqua yellowwood is the king of the trees in the forest. The bush is inhabited by baboon, leopard, lynx, bushpig, porcupine, buck and a host of other animals.

Apart from the vast indigenous forests, which offer a range of classic hikes and trails, the Knysna area contributes over 8000 plant species to the Cape floral kingdom, a wonderland of amazing plants that spread from the West Coast, across the Cape, all the way up the East Coast.

Perhaps because of this rustic paradise, the people are mellow and hospitable. The population includes a high proportion of craftsmen and artists, who work with wood, fabric and products from the sea. In some of the outlying forests, communes of hippies chill out in cosmic union, a little like Nimbin, near Byron Bay in New South Wales, Australia.

As the tourist sites put it, Knysna offers a temperate climate, a fine selection of accommodation, restaurants and adventure activities that make it the perfect holiday destination. It also has access to a range of surf spots in the Southern Cape, and is within easy striking distance of the rich surfing area of Cape St Francis and Jeffrey's Bay, a mere two hours' drive away.

THE HEADS ** ■ ◰

There is actually a surf spot just inside the Knysna Heads, believe it or not. A small group of locals ride it quite often. On a low tide with a solid swell running outside the cliffs, the sand bars here gladly accept fun and hollow 3–4' waves. The fun is tempered with the knowledge that you have to paddle all the way across the channel to the other side, often when the tide is pushing in through the heads. Incidentally, the Knysna Heads is one of only two places in the world where vessels won't be insured by Lloyds shipping agents. This adds a bit more spice to a daring dash across the channel.

THOSE WERE THE DAYS...THOSE WERE THE DAYS...THOSE WERE THE

We did uncover that Robinson Crusoe existence there. The point was the most electric blue every day we surfed it and the locals sat and watched us from the beach as we surfed. We met one whose name was Roger or James or something as equally unlikely.

He was nine years old, wore baggies and a T-shirt and was constantly as stoned as a rock garden. We decided that we didn't want to take him up on his offer to sell us some of his dope, it just didn't seem right getting stoned when we could have been surfing. And, maybe just as well.

We stayed for days at Coffee Bay, surfing, chilling, hiking around the area and battling the meanest, kamikaze, son-of-a-bitch mosquitoes I've ever seen. Fred and Chris took to smearing themselves with garlic to keep the beasts at bay, I just couldn't resort to such a savage remedy and spent the nights at least in the assurance that I was safe from the vampires with my companions nearby.

Eventually we left Coffee Bay and made for Port Edward. I'd been there about 10 years before and remembered camping near the river. We crossed the suspension

Stilbaai, p. 96.

Secret reef

ROBBERG ★★ ● 🏖 👑

The break at Robberg, the protruding headland at Plett, needs a southeasterly swell to break. It's a combination of rocks and sand. Robberg is inconsistent, but gets fairly good occasionally.

THE WRECK ★★★ ■ 🏖

Not to be confused with the Wedge (below), the Wreck is also a wedge, but with a lot more going for it, when it breaks, that is. Not as consistent, but a much longer ride and better form. The Wreck is in the corner just on the east side of Robberg. Similar to Dunes – which probably makes it the best beachbreak wave around Plett. Does need a monster swell to wrap in, or a more southerly or southeasterly swell. Waves bounce off the peninsula and peak off the wreck forming wicked A-frame barrels.

THE WEDGE ★★★ ■ 🏖

In sight of a large tourist hotel (the Beacon Isle) built on an outcrop of rocks in Plettenberg Bay, the Wedge breaks on the sand close to shore in the left corner of the beach. It gets insanely hollow and powerful for its size. Swells bounce off some rocks and head parallel to the beach to bump into other oncoming swells, creating the wedge. Not all the waves wedge up in this way. However, if they don't, it usually means a closeout because the wave breaks too close to shore. A short but zippy little barrel can provide lots of fun in the right conditions, low tide and a clean 3–4' swell.

bridge back into our beloved homeland, but couldn't find a turn-off to take us down to the river's edge. So we turned around heading back towards the Kei again. Pretty soon we realised there obviously wasn't a turn-off and we were about to reach the border post again. Fred was driving and he pulled off to the roadside and swung a U-turn. Off to the side, in the bushes, a figure came barreling towards us. He was dressed in cammo with a Port Jackson bush for a hat and he came to a halt in the road in front of us, his right hand resting on the 9 mil on his hip and his left greeting us in a tribute to Hitler.

I for one, kakked myself, and I know Fred and Chris were not far off in their reaction to our predicament. We pictured ourselves thrown away into rotten prisons like that guy in Midnight Express. The Rambo in our headlights was sure to find the kilo of coke which had materialized in the cubby hole, the haul of dope in the boot, the RPGs in the surfboard covers. He approached Fred's window with that smug, 'jy's nou busted' routine that we all know so well. 'Good evening sir, why are you turning around from the Border Post?' I could sense the subtext of Fred's reply; 'because the idiot

LOOKOUT BEACH ★★ ● ◻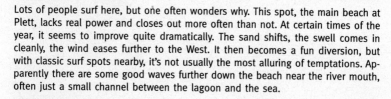

Lots of people surf here, but one often wonders why. This spot, the main beach at Plett, lacks real power and closes out more often than not. At certain times of the year, it seems to improve quite dramatically. The sand shifts, the swell comes in cleanly, the wind eases further to the West. It then becomes a fun diversion, but with classic surf spots nearby, it's not usually the most alluring of temptations. Apparently there are some good waves further down the beach near the river mouth, often just a small channel between the lagoon and the sea.

KEURBOOMS ★★★★ ■ ◻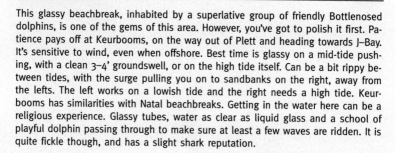

This glassy beachbreak, inhabited by a superlative group of friendly Bottlenosed dolphins, is one of the gems of this area. However, you've got to polish it first. Patience pays off at Keurbooms, on the way out of Plett and heading towards J–Bay. It's sensitive to wind, even when offshore. Best time is glassy on a mid-tide pushing, with a clean 3–4' groundswell, or on the high tide itself. Can be a bit rippy between tides, with the surge pulling you on to sandbanks on the right, away from the lefts. The left works on a lowish tide and the right needs a high tide. Keurbooms has similarities with Natal beachbreaks. Getting in the water here can be a religious experience. Glassy tubes, water as clear as liquid glass and a school of playful dolphin passing through to make sure at least a few waves are ridden. It is quite fickle though, and has a slight shark reputation.

...THOSE WERE THE DAYS...THOSE WERE THE DAYS...THOSE WERE THE

moron in the back said that this was the way to the campsite.' 'Uh, cos, ah, we were looking for the road to the campsite?' Fred ventured hopefully. 'Would you all step out of the vehicle,' he offered in reply.

Oh jeez, I hope we don't get gang raped in prison. 'Would you open the trunk of your vehicle please.' As the lid was lifted, Rambo could barely contain his delight at beholding two, fully-stuffed, black rubbish bags. 'Open up those bags please,' he was an awfully polite paratrooper.

Fark, I wonder what they'll feed us in prison. Rambo was so chuffed with himself. In his eyes you could see the reflection of his thoughts, the headline, promotion...

Fred opened one bag, then the other. We were as relieved as Rambo was bitterly disappointed to discover that the bags were stuffed with our soggy wetsuits. He checked twice, maybe to see if the seams were sewn with hemp or something.

Rambo reluctantly let us go and we drove off towards Port Edward looking for a sign that said campsite, or maybe one that said pub/kroeg.

This area is the soul of surfing in South Africa. A land of aloes, dolphins, perfect points and classic reefs. The area around Cape St Francis, Jeffrey's Bay and Port Elizabeth is part of the Eastern Cape. However, the quality of the waves makes it worthy of a special mention. Flanked by mountains to the northwest and the ocean to the southeast, this coastline is the transition between the southern Cape and the eastern Cape. The coast is beginning to curve towards the northeast, rather than travelling due east.

The J-Bay lineup.

The landscape is flat and relatively dry between the sea and the mountains. Vegetation is characterised by aloes, fleshy sour figs (good for jellyfish stings), Cape fynbos and shrubland. Distant views of steely blue mountains and the vast bays that characterise Jeffrey's Bay and Algoa Bay, make for beautiful landscapes. A glassy afternoon at Supers can be a divine experience, especially when the dolphins make their appearance, darting in and out of the waves right next to you; showing us what surfing is all about.

OYSTER BAY ** ■ ⌐ ᨊ

A fickle, exposed beachbreak. The sand shifts and it's sensitive to wind. Best in light N-NE winds and a clean medium-sized groundswell (3–5').

SEAL POINT **** ■ ᨊ

Seal Point, or 'Seals', with its landmark lighthouse, is a point with two distinct sections: an outside and a fullstop rock, from where the inside breaks. The inside is a more common phenomenon, except during peak surfing season between April and September. The inside is a walling pointbreak on a mini-scale. It runs along a rock shelf for a good 80-100 metres.

The outside gets classic, especially if the swell swings a little more to the east, rather than directly from the southwest (the most common swell direction along the East Coast of South Africa). The swell often has to refract around the outside point before it hits Seals. It still gets good though, even when this happens, and it's not uncommon to get waves that go all the way through, past the fullstop rock and down the point. This is about a 150 metre ride.

BRUCE'S ***** ◆ ᨊ

The clean, mean, green jewel of South Africa. There are a couple of misconceptions about Bruce's. Firstly, it doesn't break that often, but does break at least 15 to 20 times a year. It's not as rare as has been made out. Secondly, when it's perfect, it does not mean it's a gentle, hotdog wave. Far from it. This wave cranks down the point at Cape St Francis like a runaway steam train. When it grinds, it growls and spits. The drop at big Bruce's is a stomach churner. And slotting into the gaping barrel is a dice with a thick, thudding lip metres from a jagged line of rocks. They're all the same depth. They're all at a similar angle to the line of swell, creating that perfect consistency in movement. To feast your eyes on these grinding tubes is to see one of the wonders of the world! See you in the green room.

CAPE ST FRANCIS **** ● ⌐

Some excellent peaks along the beach. Best in broken easterly swells and light W–NW offshore breezes.

CLAPTON'S COILS ***** ◆ ᨊ

A long paddle out to this classic left-hand pointbreak. It's in front of a rivermouth somewhere near Aston Bay. It gets superlative in the right conditions, but you have to know when. Only the locals do. Picks up more swell than Supers. Needs light NW breezes and easterly swell.

Named after a store owner who provided victuals to seafarers in 1849, Jeffrey's Bay has evolved into a bustling holiday centre. About 25 years ago, Jeffrey's was a quiet, undiscovered fishing village. In the 60s, holidaymakers discovered the beautiful beaches. Then a small band of surfers found tubular nirvana at the Point, a couple of stops down from the main peak, Supertubes, which was then considered too fast to surf.

The community of J–Bay is now driven by surfing, the core economic activity, followed by fishing, property development and tourism. In the off-season, there isn't much to do. Some might even consider it boring. The population has strong representation by conservative Afrikaans folk. However, the locals wouldn't have it any other way. Besides, if a spring or autumn swell arrives: more waves, less hassle.

Like nearby St Francis, J–Bay is a holiday destination for locals accommodated by numerous caravan parks, campsites, self-catering chalets and hotels. Jeffrey's Bay overflows with holidaymakers during the summer. In winter, hordes of surfers descend from all corners of the globe. Apart from the perfect barrelling walls of Supertubes, Tubes and the Point – the three main sections along the point – Jeffrey's Bay offers other aspects worthy of mention.

Each high tide deposits on the beach a sparkling treasure of shells, including cone, nautilus, cowrie, conch, harp and pansy. They are often in perfect condition and are a collector's pot of gold. Dolphins, whales, seals and chokka (squid) are common in the area.

When the sun rises, casting its golden hue over the sea and lighting up the misty Elandsberg mountains in the distance, schools of dolphins stop by on their feeding route. When there are waves, they turn on an exhibition of free surfing, like no human could ever hope to emulate. Streaking beneath and above the waves, these grey torpedoes are an exhilarating combination of grace and power. Good wave selection too. If you are lucky to be sitting in the lineup at dawn when the waves are a perfect 4–6', a light offshore is blowing and the dolphins give you a glimpse of their inside circle, you have been witness to one of nature's most exquisite moments. Bear it in mind when screaming blue murder at the guy who ruined your perfect wall during the weekend bunfight.

KITCHEN WINDOWS **** ■

As you enter Jeffrey's Bay, there are a number of spots surfed by locals and little by anyone else. Unless you spend a fair amount of time in J–Bay, Kitchen Windows won't be on your itinerary. You'll probably spend most of your time salivating over the prospect of surfing Supertubes. In fact, you will go surfing in mushy, 2' slop at Supers, oblivious to the fact that Kitchen Windows is cooking with clean 2–4' waves. Not as powerful as other spots.

MAGNA TUBES ★★★★ ◆

The reef slightly around the corner from Supers. In front of the Beach Hotel. Fast and hard-breaking off an exposed reef, left and right. Closes out often, but best when the swell is small. Picks up more swell than Supers.

BONEYARDS ★★★★★ ◆

Occy in his former heyday ruled this spot for extended periods of the surf season. To go right is to negotiate a hectically fast wall that barrels in varying sections towards the main take-off zone at Supertubes. To make it through these sections, especially backhand, is a noble feat. It's even possible to take off at outside Boneyards, fly through some heartstopping barrels and exit right at Supertubes, then scream obscenities at the numerous jealous surfers trying to drop in on you.

Boneyards works differently at different sizes. When it's generally flat, and there's hardly a ripple at Supers, Boneyards can get a few 3' waves. In these, and slightly bigger conditions, you can go left as well as right.

SUPERTUBES ★★★★★ ◆

Probably South Africa's longest and most consistently good wave. We're talking quality and power, with an almost divine ability to loosen up surfers with the stiffest, most ungainly styles. It's ordained by ocean deities as a mecca for surf. It began in the late 60s and early 70s parallel to places like Torquay in Oz, which is near Bells Beach. Both were hippie hangouts from whence came the surf dynasties: Rip Curl, Billabong, Country Feeling and others.

When on the beach or in the water, you can feel the magic. The rock formations, the shells, the dolphins, the distant mountains, the texture of the ocean, the birds, and line upon line of grooved ocean, delivering cylinder after cylinder of perfect surf. It works best in a southwesterly swell that wraps into the bay. In terms of size, you can get perfect waves anywhere from 2' to 12', depending on swell direction. The swell can come up within hours from totally flat to 8'. Supertubes is best in a southwesterly or westerly wind. The northwester, which is usually a good offshore wind for many east coast spots, is cross-shore at J–Bay. It gives the sea a nasty bumpy texture, and locals call it the Devil's Wind.

In a solid 8' swell, with the right conditions, you are more likely to ride all the way down the point, to or even past Impossibles, even past the Point, if you pick up one of the bigger 'sidewinders' that wrap around the point more to the left. The meat of the wave is further down and somehow this prevents it closing out when it hits Impossibles. However, it also commits you to pulling into one of the most awesome barrels of your life. As Impossibles approaches, locals or seasoned visitors will raise both arms in the air and point down the point. It's a signal to whoever is interested, that the person is going for broke, all the way down. Then it's time to build up speed by drawing lines near the top of the feathering wall. As you

J-Bay locals.

Dolphins

Our entire coastline is blessed with several species of both porpoise and dolphin. Pods appear frequently, particularly in the Eastern Cape and KwaZulu-Natal. The most prevalent species are the Bottlenose, Dusky and Common dolphin. Visitors to Jeffrey's Bay are awestruck when watching the local Bottlenose dolphin crew racing down the long, walling cylinders of Supertubes at high speed and ramping into the air out of the back of the waves.

Another classic dolphin hangout lies between Umhlanga and Zinkwazi Beach in KwaZulu-Natal, otherwise known as the Dolphin Coast. The Humpbacked dolphin is found here. These shy creatures are more elusive than their cold water cousins.

Dolphins are friendly. They often play 'chicken' with surfers sitting in the lineup. When you see the trademark dorsal fins rolling towards you, slip under water and watch them speed past you, sometimes only metres away.

Berg winds

A direct offshore wind that smoothes the ocean into perfect surfing conditions, depending on the angle of the spot. Jeffrey's Bay, for instance, is cross-shore in a NW berg wind. Locals call it 'Devil's Wind'. Generally, the berg wind is sought after. Berg winds often precede a cold front. The berg wind is warm and dry. On the West Coast, it blows from the NE and on the East Coast, it blows from the NW.

begin to reach critical mass, short of taking off into the air, you drop into the bowl and hang on for an eternity. Deep in the pit, the sunlight recedes until it becomes what seems like a speck in front of you, like the exit to a round blue cave where daylight is a distant glare. Oh no, this is it, too deep! But hey, suddenly the entrance draws back. It hovers once or twice, flirting, before peeling back over your head. You're in the sunlight. It's good to be alive. Some dudes at Tubes are staring. You don't care. You're shaking with sheer ecstasy. You kick out, even though you could have carried on. What's the point in surfing through the Point? You've just had the wave of your life. Time to get out, and walk all the way back up to Supers along the beach, about a 300 metre walk.

The flip side of J–Bay's magic aura is the crudeness of building developments mushrooming everywhere. Ugly houses have hurt the old Jeffrey's Bay. The Supers carpark has shrunk. The famous aloes that lined the pristine bush along the point have been mostly herded into a plantation as part of a dune reclamation project. Hordes of foreign surfers, clutching strong currency, descend on J–Bay to enjoy cheap surf holidays. They often stay for months-on-end, getting into the stoke of surfing one of the best waves on our planet. However, treat this wave, and the locals, with respect, otherwise you will come off second best.

SALAD BOWLS ★★★★ ◆

At the end of Impossibles lies a short barrelling section called Salad Bowls. It's not really an official spot along the point, but some people refer to it as such.

TUBES ★★★★★ ■

Fast-breaking section past Salad Bowls and Impossibles. A classic wave that's slightly more forgiving, but not much. Shows the same superlative form as Supers, but not as fast. All the waves along this stretch are offshore in a southwesterly wind.

THOSE WERE THE J–BAY DAYS

By Laurence Platt

In 1964, when you drove to Jeffrey's Bay from Cape Town, up the Garden Route, you knew when you were close to the mecca. The climate changed. You knew you were getting close. It was an indescribable feeling. Like moving into another climate zone. And the scent. The pungent aroma of the Jeffrey's fynbos. That unique scent of J-Bay.

In the beginning, there were just waves, later came the development, the houses and the parking lots.

But in the beginning there was just the land abutting the point. No 9' 6" board could have made it through 'tubes' or 'supertubes' (although we did not have those names back then) so no one bothered to try.

Anthony ('Ant') van den Heuvel 'owned' Jeffrey's Bay point back then, and almost every (longboard) surfer in South Africa, at that time, knew all the other surfers in the country on a first name basis. Many of the

POINT ***** ■ ⌒ ⌒

Further down from Supers, past Impossibles, Salad Bowls and Tubes, lies the Point. It's about two thirds of the way down the length of the point from the outside peak at Supertubes. It's a mellower version of Supers, but still walls up fairly fast and offers a couple of fun barrel sections. Gets perfect. Lacks the adrenalin rush – and fierce competition – that you get further up the point.

ALBATROSS **** ● ⌒ ⌒

The last stop in a long line of sections along the point at J–Bay. Some surfers have been known to surf all the way from Boneyards to, and through, Albatross. After that, you run out of ocean and it's physically impossible to surf further. Having said that, it's fair to say that the length of this ride could be about 1,2 km. That's 1,200 metres. Think about it: two rides and you have ridden 2,4 km. Albatross is a smaller and mellower version of Point.

....PORT ELIZABETH

The Friendly City, the fifth biggest in South Africa, is also called the Windy City, because it is often regaled by howling SW winds. However, as suggested by its first name, the people are hospitable, the beaches are sheltered and the nightlife varied and fun. Because Algoa Bay is located on the southeastern tip of the country, it juts out enough to cop the savage westerly winds that blast across the top of the southern storms that sweep past to the south, from West to East.

The city is located along the southwestern corner of the bay. It was here that many 1820 settlers laid down their roots. One can see a lot of graceful, period architecture mixed in with a bustling modern city.

Port Elizabeth, called PE by South Africans, is a mere 45-minute drive from

OLD J–BAY...THE OLD J–BAY...THE OLD J–BAY...THE OLD J–BAY...THE

faces in the South African chapter of Bruce Brown's film *The Endless Summer* were friends of mine.

We drove our Volkswagen Kombis and Beetles and Austin Mini Minors, replete with roofracks, with about six boards lashed to each, down the dirt road to Jeffrey's Bay village. There was no 'official' parking lot at the point. There was no construction at the point. Just sand dunes. The locals townsfolk did not know they lived near some of the most amazing waves on the planet.

But the friendly farmer who owned the land at the point knew what we were there for (even though he may have 'checked us skew' at first). After the first few visits, he even installed a solitary tap, so that we could get fresh water.

If we did not sleep in the kombis, we slept in the bushes on the dunes. We braided the 6' tall gorse into habitable 'units' and stayed there for weeks on end – each respecting our neighbours who inhabited a similar braided unit on the dune. Before sunrise we were all awake – listening for

Jeffrey's Bay. It offers a huge range of accommodation, from Bed and Breakfasts (often converted homes), to five star hotels. There are also numerous backpacker hotels.

The city is lucky to have three open areas within its confines: Donkin Reserve, St George's Park and Settler's Park. Historically, there is quite a lot to see and do in the area. You're quite close to the Cango Caves, the Addo Elephant Park and great hiking trails.

WILD SIDE ★★★★★ ■ ⌂ ⌄

Plenty of excellent options on the south side of Algoa Bay, along the stretch of coast that faces more directly into the prevailing SW swells. The swell is always bigger here, but is sensitive to the wind. The SW, which is so good for most of the Eastern Cape pointbreaks, is cross-shore here. Best conditions are light NW berg-winds and a clean 2–6' groundswell. Several secret reefs get epic along the wild side, even when the NE is blowing, which is offshore at some spots. However, to get the best out of this coastline, you'll have to infiltrate the local PE community.

Coming from the West along the wild side travelling from Van Stadensmond, there are several nature reserves, such as the Maitland Mines Nature Reserve and the Island Forest Reserve and Seaview Game Park.

This stretch of coast includes a host of classic surf spots, such as Maitlands, Beachview, Seaview, Craters, Virgin Bay, Rocky's, Sardinia Bay, Main Rights, Bullets, Secrets, and Non Kom.

NOORDHOEK ★★★★ ■ ⌂ ⌄

A right-hand beachbreak and reef combined. Direct offshore is NW. Doesn't handle big swell. Best in light NW, 2–4' swell and a low tide.

the break even before it was light enough to see it.

In those days, for ten cents you could by a half a pint of milk, a loaf of course meal brown bread and half a dozen bananas at the village cafe. This was supplemented by the sea snail 'alikruikels', which we dove out of the bay from our surfboards in between sets and cooked in their shells over open flames. It was a nutritious meal fit for kings. At night, lit by the fires of piles of driftwood, we shared the stories of the day's 'kraakers' – not that there was any-

thing unknown. Everyone there had been in the water at the same time.

Some things never change. If you have heard the crash of the waves at Jeffrey's as they hit the rocks, you will know that you are not just listening to a wave rising and breaking. You are listening to a wave which rises and then smashes 'with intention' – like a freight train careening down the point.

And even when the sun has set, you can tell that the freight train waves are still there as they rumble down the point until

Bruce's Beauties, p. 110.

PE wildside, p. 116.

SUMMERSTRAND ** ⬤ 🏠

A fairly consistent beachbreak that works best when its in the 2–5' region. Breaks left and right, and prefers a westerly or light southwesterly wind. Sand banks tend to shift around.

MILLERS POINT *** ■ 🏠 👑

This right-hander gets good occasionally. Half a pointbreak and half a beachbreak, it needs big, south swells and light W winds. Often a bit 'pap', or weak, but can be reasonably good in an easterly swell, which comes on to the break more directly.

THE FENCE **** ◆ 🏠

A hollow wedging beachbreak that is one of PE's most popular spots. Left and right peaks. Works in a 2–6' groundswell in westerly winds. Can go off in summer on NE swells followed by the SW.

PIPE *** ■ 🏠

The Pipe can be fickle, but it's a wedging, hollow little wave at its best in 3–4' groundswell that has wrapped into Algoa Bay from the south. It turns on in an easterly swell, but is known for being inconsistent. Gets blown out easily.

There are many more spots along this coastline that have not been mentioned. Do some exploring, it will definitely be worth it.

you fall asleep dreaming of tomorrow ... and how you can perfect that 'toes on the nose' manoeuvre you almost got right today.

Jeffrey's Bay (we did not call it 'J–Bay' back then) is still there. But the dunes and the land have been changed. Houses and business sites have been built, and the solitary water tap has gone.

But the waves are there. Endless. Churning. Cranking. The Green Room. That's still there.

Many years from now, when all the houses and parking lots are overgrown ruins and the developments have been washed away, the waves will still be there.

And the eternal Green Room will still be calling me.

J–bay, a different perspective.

Seal Point beachbreak, p. 110.

The Eastern Cape is often regarded as the most consistent surfing coastline in South Africa. It has the best of everything. Not as cold as the Southern Cape and not as hot as KwaZulu-Natal, the Eastern Cape gets swell from the southern cold fronts, and enjoys solid wind swells and cyclone swells emanating from the Mozambique channel to the northeast. The climate is dominated by the Agulhas Current, often pulling warm water from the tropical zones of the Mozambique Channel. This keeps water temperatures cool in winter and warm in summer, often reaching 22°C.

Summers can be hot and humid from Port Alfred northwards into the East London and Transkei area, while the winters can get cold when fierce fronts lash

So many waves, so little time.

the coast. However, temperate conditions mostly apply. The winters are mostly mild, especially the autumn months between March and May. The weather is warm, with more sunshine than further south, because the fronts have often faded before they reach this coast.

Strong cold fronts sometimes bring cold snaps and bad weather, with SW winds and cold rainy days. But then, the swell gets even bigger than the consistent swells inbetween. The steeply dropping continental shelf, which runs near the shore in parts of the coast, combined with the fast-flowing currents and prevailing SW swell and wind have been known to create huge groundswell conditions on the coast, in the 20'+ range, with freak swells of 60' twenty miles offshore.

KELLY'S BEACH ★★ ● ⊏▱

The surf rats of Port Alfred cut their teeth on this wave, building their skills to the level required to tackle the East Pier. It's a re-form that offers little in the way of juice, but lots of fun and sun-filled summer days. Jagged rocks jut from the sand in a line out to sea on the right, almost like shale. A right peaks to the left of these. Further over to the left, one can ride a few little left-hand peaks. Best when the overall swell is 4–6', which translates to about 3' on the inside at Kelly's. Fairly sensitive to the wind, Kelly's prefers a light NW or W wind.

WEST PIER ★★ ▪ ⊏▱

On the other side of the East Pier is a long beach. Alongside the pier breaks a left-hander that occasionally offers an excellent peak, it wedges up from refracting swell that has bounced off the base of the pier and rejoins swell wrapping around the pier. This wave somehow works in an onshore northeasterly, sheltered by the five metre concrete pier.

EAST PIER ★★★★★ ▪ ⊏▱

A hidden jewel. Be prepared to co–operate. You won't get this right-hander firing straight off, unless you arrive during one of those epic glassy groundswells. This spot has many faces: rugged and uncompromising, oily and smooth, or just pure barrelling filth. When the tide is low enough, the waves bowl into the mouth of the Kowie River between the two piers.

The West Pier is the longer of the two. The tip of the East Pier is rounded by a sandbank. The result is a barrelling spitting beast that hurls a thick wedgy peak into the mouth, before grinding its way past the East Pier sandbank. If the banks are lined up, the last section freight–trains across a long sandbank on the way to the beach. In optimum conditions, this wave can be world class. The wedge in the mouth gets so square, Pythagoras would be agog. In a smaller swell (and different swell direction), the waves break off the East Pier. Kowie, as its known, works best in a clean, moderate groundswell (4–6') in light NW to W winds. Some Ragged Tooth sharks — mostly bottom feeders — are occasionally caught off the West Pier.

RIET RIVER ★★★ ▪ ⊏▱ 👑

On the way out of Port Alfred, Riet River is a point with a good bowl section on the outside. However, it tends to back off down the point and can be frustrating. W winds and a clean 6' swell are optimum. Strong rips can pull you into the middle of the beach where you get the unpleasant feeling of being shark bait.

KLEINMOND ** ▪ ◻ ⚗

A sectiony right point and mediocre beachbreak. Gets quite good occasionally, but rips are strong.

MTATI ** ▪ ◻

In sight of Mpekweni casino, Mtati is tucked away on the east side of a vast beach. Some fun peaks along the beach, especially near the mouth of the Mtati River. It's privately owned though, so you'll have to walk from the hotel for about 2–3 km.

HAMBURG * ▪ ◻

Not a great spot but that's maybe because we haven't got a clue about its potential.

KIDD'S BEACH ** ● ◻

Beachbreak that looks like it has potential, but never quite does it. Moving further away from East London towards Port Alfred, this is a coastal resort where many East London families have holiday homes.

IGODA **** ▪ ◻

This sharky spot has seen a fair number of bites, bumps and other scary moments, but delivers some epic barrels. The best wave breaks near the rocks. Picks up a lot of swell, and is the spot everyone heads for when the East London breaks are bordering on too small. Happier in northerly winds, from NW to NE, and a medium easterly or southerly swell.

....EAST LONDON

EASTERN BEACH **** ▪ ◻

This spot has been known to have absolutely epic waves. However, those superlative moments are dependent on the sand banks, which build up off boulders and pebbles along the shore. It's quite fickle. You're lucky if it turns on the juice for you. Likes a clean 3–5' swell and light to moderate W winds. Lots of locals hang out here. Eastern's is near the Holiday Inn.

NAHOON REEF ***** ◆ ⚗

A world-class right-hand reef. It works in a variety of conditions and delivers a whole repertoire of different surfing combinations, depending on the size of the swell, the wind and the tide. However, at its best, the swell is 4–6', the wind is SW and the tide is low, and starting to push. A few shark attacks have occurred here, but many people still surf it. It's too good to go to waste.

CORNER **** ■ ⌃

Almost an extension of the wave at Nahoon Reef, this cranking right-hander works best when Reef is bigger. Nicely protected from the elements, Corner is popular when Reef is blown-out SW. On the best days one can ride from Nahoon Reef right through to Corner.

BONZA BAY ** ■ ⌂

Mediocre beachbreak in front of the Quinera rivermouth.

....GONUBIE BAY

There are two main waves in Gonubie proper, one off the rocks right in front of the town, and the other, a series of big lefts breaking off a point/reef on the other side of the bay, aptly called Gonubie Lefts. The lefts are more consistent but need a bigger swell. Although the waves occasionally spark, quality and consistency are not the best at these breaks. There are a series of breaks in Gonubie bay.

THE POINT ***** ■ ⌃

Hit it on the low tide and you will be hooked for life. It's a long rounded point break that peaks out at the back and halfway down. When the two waves join up, it offers the squarest tube around. Works on a small to medium swell.

MIDDLE ROCK **** ◆ ⌃

Gets dangerous. Very hollow. Works on bigger swell. Only for expert surfers.

ROCK WAVE *** ■ ⌂ ⌃

Nice little right-hander which runs along a mini-point and ends in front of a tidal pool. It's easy to ride but can get nasty when there is a large swell and the tide is high.

TIDALS ** ■ ⌂

A short barrelling wave usually ridden by bodyboarders, offering steep drops and hollow tubes.

365, Cape Peninsula.

Spot names

Surf spot names come from many sources. Some are named in a number of languages after landmarks, shipwrecks, climatic conditions, towns, rivers, beaches, mountains, people or even the shape of the wave when it breaks.

A fair number of South African spot names are part of the global surfing lexicon. The Wedge, for example, is found in a few places, including Port Elizabeth, Durban, Cape Town and Plettenberg Bay.

Then there is Pipe (PE), Supertubes, Boneyards and Impossibles (Jeffrey's Bay), Black Rock, Surfers and Tubes (KwaZulu-Natal); as well as Sunset, Sunrise, Big Bay, Off the Wall and Long Beach, found near Cape Town. They all have namesakes in California, Hawaii, Australia and Portugal, to name a few.

Many SA spots are named after the nearest geographical landmark. The Crayfish Factory is near a crayfish factory. Outer Kom is the outside reef near the town of Kommetjie, an old Dutch word meaning Little Bowl. There is also a spot called the Inner Kom.

Kowie, or East Pier, breaks in the mouth of the Kowie River off the East Pier in Port Alfred. Nahoon Reef is named after a suburb of East London called Nahoon. Battery Beach in Durban is in front of the Natal Command military base. African Beach, which was a blacks-only beach in the apartheid era, is now called Country Club. There is an element of irony to that, because the prestigious Durban Country Club is nearby.

According to some surfers, the Cape Town spot 365 was named because there is always a wave there, 365 days a year. It was allegedly first surfed in the late 60s by a big guy with red hair and a beard called Roger Bain. There is contention, however. Veteran surfer and surf shop owner Tich Paul is adamant that they gave 365 its name from the shape of the wave, which is so round, its 360 degrees plus another five. This appears to be the most accurate version. Bain was also allegedly the first to surf the Boiler (near Outer Kom), which is on top of a wreck. Others differ.

Some breaks are named after people, such as Farmer Burger's, after a local farmer who lives up the West Coast. Other spots are named after nearby landmarks or a feature unique to the terrain. There are at least three breaks called Black Rock or Black Rocks: two on the North Coast (KwaZulu-Natal) one on the Cape Peninsula and another in the Eastern Cape near East London.

Long stretches of our coast, particularly the rugged Transkei Wild Coast and parts of KwaZulu-Natal are rich in ethnic heritage. Many of these spots have retained their indigenous names. In Transkei, examples include Mdumbe, Llandwile, Mbomvu and Ntlonyane. In KwaZulu-Natal, there are surf spots named Zinkwazi, Umhlali, Umhlanga and Umzumbe, mostly the names of rivers near the break. In Zulu, the prefix Um- denotes a river. 'Zumbe' is a small brown bean. Umzumbe means Small Brown Bean River.

RIVER MOUTH ★★★★

Classic beachbreak. Works on any swell direction and any wind direction. Best time to hit it is the low tide when the swell is running. If offers long right-handers and easy to ride left-handers, although the inside gets hairy at times

THE LEFTS (GONUBIE REEF) ★★★★

This wave is a classic. Works when the swell is big or small and handles most swell direction and size. It offers one of the longest rides around with a nice consistent wall.

YELLOWSANDS ★★★★★

One of the better spots in the Eastern Cape, after the obvious choices of course! Yellows comprises a point and inside beachbreak area that breaks into a small river mouth. The beachbreak has lefts and rights, depending on the way the river has deposited the sand around its mouth. The point needs specific conditions in terms of swell direction and size, and is fickle. However, it cooks sometimes. Wedgy peaks and a barrelling inside section, over the rocks, occur when the tide is high and the swell is a clean groundswell in the 6–8' region, coming from the southeast or east. Getting caught on the inside can be a bit tricky. The beachbreak copes with a stiff SW wind. Some epic hollow beachbreak peaks are common in winter.

GLEN EDEN ★★★★

Charging right-hander. It is one of few spots along this coast that work in the north-easter, the onshore that plagues the coast in summer. It needs only a small swell to break.

QUICK GUIDE TO EASTERN CAPE SURF CULTURE

By Hagen Engler

Surfers are like normal people really, with a few small exceptions. For instance, surfers are quite worried about their hair. All that time in the ocean at the mercy of the elements can leave your hair dull, lifeless and lacking body.

So although they'll seldom admit it, surfers are always scheming to themselves stuff like, 'Mmmm summer's here, that means my hair will get blonder and Jo'burg chicks'll be perving at my ass like I'm Jon Bon Jovi.' So, to look like a surfer, spend time in the sun. But since any fool can lie on a beach, go for the odd gwaf (swim) in the sea and get a tan. It's only a first step. It's very important to occasionally have saltwater dribbling out of your nose, ostensibly from taking 5' freefall wipeouts

QUEENSBERRY BAY ★★★★★ ■

This is 'The Berries', one of the choicest, juiciest waves around. It's a classic point setup, but the inside fades. However, the relatively short ride is made up by the sheer quality of the wave. Can handle a pretty big swell, in the 10' category. The swell walls up along a shallow rock shelf around the corner of the point. In glassy conditions it can be classic. The rides tend to get a bit longer, the bigger the swell. An easterly push to the swell also helps. Needs a light NW wind. Doesn't like the SW wind, unless it's a gentle breeze. Nice place to stay with caravan park, camping sites and bungalows. Quiet during the week.

CINTSA WEST ★★ ■

Average pointbreak with steep take off, but fades fairly quickly. Needs a solid swell and winter offshores.

CINTSA EAST ★★★ ■

Another below-par beachbreak. However, it's been known to spark occasionally. Best during clean winter swells and light offshore, westerly winds. Follow signs from East Coast resorts. Keep heading northeast, parallel to the coast.

HAGA-HAGA ★★ ■

Not great for surfing. There is a left point in front of the hotel. Bit rippy. There is also a reef. Haga-Haga is a classic little place, perhaps the first proper Wild Coast resort. The hotel is quaint, friendly and right on the beach. An advantage is its proximity to the city of East London — although the roads are bad — and the range of great surf spots in the area.

at the Fence. The principle is more or less like a nasal enema. Water goes up, stays there for a while and then runs out a while later, usually when you look down to check your fly, or when speaking to someone you've just met. Very authentic. It can be replicated using syringes, bicycle pumps or perhaps by doing handstands in the shower.

Red eyes are another great surfer disguise. These are from squinting into the spray coming off the back of the waves on windy days. That and erm, bright sun. To get red eyes, put brake fluid, Tabasco or polyester resin catalyst in them. Or have someone smack you really hard in the face. Voila! Red eyes, runny nose, and a flushed expression not dissimilar to sunburn.

Further, surfers talk funny. This is basically from hanging out with the same people all the time. In much the same way as groups of people who go on three-week

DOUBLE MOUTH ★★★ ■ ⌂

A right-hand reefbreak just to the south of Morgan's Bay. It breaks into a channel. Best on moderate south swells with a light NW. Good camping area. Check it out from the top of the hill.

MORGAN'S BAY ★★★ ● ⌂

Another quaint resort that comes alive in the season over Christmas. The Eastern Cape is peppered with these small towns that are basically dead during the off-season, but cook when all the townies, from as far afield as Gauteng, arrive for the summer holidays. Unfortunately, most of them don't offer really excellent surf, apart from a few notable exceptions! Morgan's Bay is an exposed beachbreak that works in small swell and light offshores.

BARBEL POINT ★★★ ■ ⌂

Another right point. Offers more juice than the spots to it's immediate north. There's a more defined lineup, although the sections only connect when the swell is big enough and coming from the right direction. Needs a large, clean south swell and SW winds. Best when a coastal low pulls into the area.

WHACKY POINT ★★★★★ ◆ ⌂

Right-hand pointbreak and beach that is fairly fickle, but when it works it could be compared to some of the best waves in the country. It is not a spot that is surfed too often by the East London locals due to the condition of the road to Kei Mouth. Can get perfect. At least two barrel sections on the wave – if you are natural. Backhand – not so easy.

QUICK GUIDE TO SURF CULTURE...QUICK GUIDE TO SURF CULTURE...

holidays come back hating each other but talking an esoteric language and laughing about things no-one else understands.

Also, surfers are always on the lookout for new words to incorporate into their dictionary. So you can always fake it by making up your own words. Say something like, 'Aaaayowzissekse? Ou sckims fully Noncom (*surf spot in PE*) as it pushes, but it's summer banks broe. And that's a long pull, hey, and I'm tuning, 'Roots, it's gonna be roots,' but we pull in and, ay, less sand. It's only acid, hey. Scheming how's zis, hey. Sucks broe.' Also the phrase, 'Gettinganywaveslatelyyay?' is pronounced as one word, as shown above. The right answer to this question is 'Ay less, hey,' in summer, and 'Fully. Supers going off on Thursday, broe,' in wintertime.

The final touch is the surfer walk, also known as dwindling. Dwindling is similar to the, 'going for your morning pee after you

Gonubie Lefts, p. 124.

Queensberry Bay, p. 127.

WHISPERING WAVES ★★★ ■

Right pointbreak to the west of Kei Mouth. Another marginal wave. Tends to be a bit 'pap', lacking in power. Best on small swells with a SW wind. Lots of seaweed in the lineup.

PERIWINKLES ★★★★★ ■ ◻

One of the best spots in the area, say several of the locals. Periwinkles breaks on a shallow rock shelf quite close to the shore. It works on easterly and southeasterly swells but needs a light to moderate NW wind. It needs a low tide, otherwise it becomes a rocky shorebreak. It's close to the small town of Weymouth. Said locals are adamant that it deserves five stars for quality.

KEI MOUTH ★★ ■ ◻

A marginal wave at this small village, with many holiday shacks and a small hotel, which marks the old border between South Africa and Transkei. It's a left and right peaking beachbreak. Best on easterly swell and a warm NW wind. Not great, but Kei Mouth is not a bad place to hang out for a while. Plenty of surf further south. During the holiday season in December and January, Kei Mouth is a favourite hangout for school-leavers and university students, and has a carnival atmosphere, although on a small, rural scale. If you prefer the bustle of Times Square to celebrate New Year, then you can miss out Kei Mouth.

drank half of a brewery the night before and you're not sure if you're up, or if you're just gonna have the pee and go back to doss,' walk. Aimlessness is the key to the dwindle.

Only trips to the beach are goal-orientated, if you're walking anywhere else, look like you're not quite sure where you're going. If you're dwindling with other people, turn to them every now and then and go, 'So where we going, ay?'

And that's all there is to it. You might also consider buying a surfboard, although this might be overkill.

Another empty lineup.

Yellowsands, p. 126.

WILD COAST

During the days of apartheid the Transkei was a 'homeland', a reservoir of cheap labour for the apartheid machine. Today, it is officially part of the Eastern Cape, but is still known as Transkei, or the 'Kei' among surfers. It denotes a special region that offers classic surf holidays and amazing surf sessions in remote, rural locations, with herdboys and cows to keep you company.

When you head to the Kei, home of South Africa's choicest dope and birthplace of Nelson Mandela, it's like stepping into another dimension. Everything becomes laid-back and rustic. It's easy to fall prey to 'Pondoland fever', a condition of great lethargy that can befall a visitor. This has something to do with the warm climate,

Pointbreaks along the rugged Transkei coast.

rural lifestyle, relaxed locals and its illegal crops! The weather is mostly fine all year around, although in the summer rainy season it gets humid and hot. Transkei is dry in winter, when the best surf occurs. This is a good time to visit, when big groundswell arrives from the fronts that batter the southern Cape. Transkei is also far less sharky, because the rivers subside and don't flood the ocean with dirty river water strewn with debris.

Facilities and amenities are often rudimentary, except those found in small towns that house a resort or a number of hotels, such as Mazeppa Bay, Coffee Bay, Hole-in-the-Wall, Trennerys, Mngazi, Presley's Bay and Port St Johns.

MAZEPPA BAY ★★ ◼ ⌁

Another laid–back Transkei resort. Friendly staff. Good food. Cold beer. The only problem is, not many waves. There is a short right-hander near the island and a left that breaks into a rip on the east side. Lots of explorative potential, providing you have a four-wheel drive vehicle.

NTLONYANE (BREEZY POINT) ★★★★★ ◆ ⌁

Unfortunately this classic pointbreak has gained notoriety as one of the worst places in South Africa for shark attacks. Several surfers have lost their lives here. Nevertheless, it is probably the most consistent spot along the entire Wild Coast. It's a long, tubing right-hand pointbreak, similar to J–Bay. The best conditions are in a large southerly swell, and southwesterly winds. To minimise the risk of shark attack, make sure you don't visit during the peak summer months, when the rivers are swollen with rains that wash a lot of muck into the sea. During winter, which is more consistent for surf anyway, this spot is definitely worth a visit.

MPAME ★★ ◼ ⌁

Not a great surf spot. There is a right-hander off the point into a deep channel here. It's best on a southerly swell and light northwesterly winds.

SHARPLEYS REEF ★★ ◼ ⌂ ⌁

A rocky pointbreak with sectiony rights. Best in a southerly swell when the waves wrap on to the sand bank. Turn off to the south from the Coffee Bay road, and follow gravel roads along the river. Also check Mncwasa Point to the north.

HOLE–IN–THE–WALL ★★ ● ⌂

At the main beach, to the left of the famous hole, a free-standing sandstone cliff with a truck-sized hole in the middle, is a fun beachbreak. Not surfed all that much, but it is fun for the novelty value.

MBOMVU ★★★ ◼ ⌁

The next bay to the right of Coffee Bay, this little wave goes off, but only at certain times of the year. Sometimes it doesn't work at all. When it's all lined up, you surf a small sand bank and pebble setup, breaking right just away from a small river. Very hollow and fun wave. Best at 2–4' in a westerly breeze. This wave can go for several years without working, and suddenly come right for a few months.

..........COFFEE BAY

So named when a ship returning to Europe from the East, carrying a cargo of coffee beans, was washed up on the beach. Apparently several of the seeds took root and for a time coffee trees grew.

Coffee Bay has undergone many changes. It used to be a small coastal haven for store owners and businessmen from Umtata and East London, who built small shacks there. Nowadays, it has a couple of backpackers hotels, a country store, a hotel and one of the best campsites in the country: each unit is a private, hollowed out space in a grove of Milkwood and other indigenous trees. One of the two old hotels, The Ocean View, is still operating. The other, The Lagoon Hotel, has fallen into disrepair.

The bay, between the Mbomvu and Nenga rivers, is particularly beautiful. Flanked on the left by rocky cliffs and on the right by a mellow point that runs along a thin slab of rocks, Coffee Bay is a great spot to spend a week or two. There are some good waves to be had on the beach and on the point, with several waves in the area, which work at various times of the year, mostly in winter.

The main thing about Coffee Bay, however, is that it can be used as a base to check out the area. It is near Umtata Mouth, an hour's walk to the northeast, which is great for fishing (several deepsea boats launch from here) and exploring. Coffee Bay is a two–hour walk from Hole-in-the-Wall to the southwest, where nature has created an extremely unusual rock formation: a giant slab of rock with a hole right through it. The lagoon here is magical. Travellers can also use Coffee Bay as a base to go on various surf missions.

COFFEE BAY POINT ★★★ ■

A mellow and fun right-hand point on the right side of Coffee Bay. The take-off zone occurs over a small rock shelf. The wave then peels to the right and breaks along rocks. Best at 2–4' in westerly winds, the point can handle slightly bigger conditions if the swell has more of an easterly push to it. In a normal southerly swell, much of the swell energy is expended on an outer point, before reforming and refracting around the point and lining up again on the inside. The length of the ride depends on the sand banks further down the point, where a small stream enters the sea. At certain times of the year, it gets good.

COFFEE BAY BEACH ★★★ ■ ▭

There are a number of peaks to the left of the small river mouth that come out at the base of the point. In light westerly or northwesterly conditions at about 3–6', the beach can deliver incredibly good waves, particularly the lefts that break towards the river mouth. It is similar to Yellowsands near East London.

MAPUZI ** ■ ⌂ 灬

This right-hander, which breaks off the edge of a rock shelf and then grinds across a river mouth, is not surfed often on account of it being a fickle wave, and due to the abundance of sharks in the area (fishermen often catch them off a small hill that juts into the ocean nearby).

WHALE ROCK *** ◆ 灬

Short, fast and hollow reef. Best in small to moderate southerly swells and calm glassy conditions. Whale Rock is around the point to the south of Mdumbe, where a large sandstone rock sticks out of the water.

MDUMBE ***** ◆ ⌂ 灬

The hardcore jewel of the Wild Coast. Yet another perfect point. This time, a little more gnarly, and, when conditions and sand banks are lined up, this wave can break for an incredible 500–800 metres, depending on whether or not you make the last freight train section across the river–mouth sand banks. Mdumbe is best at about 6–10' in a moderate westerly or southwesterly wind. When at its superlative best, Mdumbe rivals Jeffrey's Bay. However, it's much more difficult to get to, and has rudimentary facilities, a petty crime problem and the inevitable shark presence. There is a camp site nearby. The paddle out can be a bit daunting because the only way to get out is through a deep crevice in the rocks. The only problem is that when you lower yourself into the channel, your view of the oncoming sets is blocked. You need a wave spotter to stand on the rocks and give you the thumbs-up when there is a lull.

PONDOLAND FEVER...PONDOLAND FEVER...PONDOLAND FEVER...POND

PONDOLAND FEVER

By an anonymous traveller

Once, as a hiker, I took a trip through the luscious Transkei and discovered a perfect surf spot.

Imagine 280 kilometres of coastal wilderness on your back doorstep. A land where, apart from the odd Coke can and transistor radio, people live as they did hundreds of years ago. There are few phones, roads are bad and disease is rife. There are also mystical pointbreaks, lurching reefs and scattered beachbreaks.

We were in the middle of this land, 60 kilometres and three days walking distance from our starting point. I was the only surfer in our party of three, which was probably the only reason why I'd agreed to walk 120 kilometres of the Wild Coast.

James was the muscle, a second dan Bruce Lee with a smattering of Xhosa, something which had proven very comforting three days earlier when we'd found ourselves in a bullet-ridden taxi at Idutywa,

Sardine Run

Every winter, millions and millions of pilchards, or baby sardines, spawn off the East Coast of South Africa. They head North along the coast, enjoying the cooler Agulhas current that makes a turn down the Transkei. However, as they reach KwaZulu-Natal, the warmer Mozambique current begins to predominate. And as the water warms up, the sardines begin to panic. Millions beach themselves. It's a bonanza for human predators, who mill around, knee-deep in sea water, grabbing handfuls of sardines. It's usually pandemonium as 'old tops' (elderly people) elbow each other out of the way and fistfights break out. Following the run are hordes of other predators, such as sharks, gannets, gamefish and dolphins.

Crayfish

There are two main species of crayfish, or lobster. Along the West Coast, you find the bigger, more prevalent Cape Rock Lobster. On the East Coast in the warmer climes of the Eastern Cape and KwaZulu-Natal one finds the smaller East Coast Lobster. Strict laws apply to catching crayfish. Check with your local authority about bag limits and when the season opens.

Bluebottles

A translucent, blue jellyfish that looks like a small plastic bag. They are washed ashore along the East Coast during northeast onshore winds. They cause painful stings but are not fatal.

Bluebottle tentacles contain millions of nettle cells. If you touch them, tiny filaments shoot into your skin, releasing a toxin. A burning pain is experienced. On the scene, wash the area with sea water to remove filaments. Rinse the area with vinegar or brandy. If you don't have either, urinate on the wound. The uric acid helps. Try rubbing fleshy sour figs (vygies) – common in the Cape – on the sting. Try to soak the area in warm water. If you get to a chemist, take an anti-histamine tablet and spread cortisone on the sting.

heart of the occasional conflict. Nick was, well Nick.

The Wild Coast is majestic, but don't expect luxury from one of the poorest areas of the country. Despite the glossy hiking brochures showing homely looking rondavels, the only remnants of the rumoured hiking huts we found on the first two nights, were groups of rondavels that looked like they were victims of American smart bombs ... rings of rubble.

Cooling off around our campfire, sipping whisky on that Wednesday night, we considered ourselves lucky to have a cosy rondavel waiting, thanks to a shotgun-toting man called Wiseman, caretaker of our huts, who casually informed us that the gun was for shooting dogs. Wiseman was great; a big, round faced, jovial man. He even lent us his ten ton schooner to paddle across a river that looked too wide to swim. Only problem was James and I had to carry the thing two kilometres to the river. You guessed it, Nick was watching the bags.

We'd started out three days earlier following a narrow cattle trail on the edge of

LWANDILE ★★★★★ ◆ 🏄 👑

Another jewel of the Wild Coast. When it's going off, this is a world–class wave. Best in a southeasterly 4–6' swell and a westerly or southwesterly wind, this point-break is the perfect point / sand setup. The take-off zone is just off a slab of rock, making for a wedgy beginning to a long walling wave that sweeps past the rocks and joins a series of sand banks. As in many spots in the Kei, the length of the wave depends on the time of year and the position of the sand banks. But even when the sand banks are not perfectly set up, the point section of this wave makes for an excellent wave. When the sand flows nicely down the base of the point, you're talking about an excellent wave nearly 200 metres long. In terms of accom-modation, you can stay in nearby Presley's bay, which is on the eastern side of a long beach, or you can camp at the point or along the banks of the Lwandile River. It's best to hire a local herd-boy to stand guard at your camp while you surf. Alternatively, you can appoint a member of your group to do it. During the day, you can cool off in a small, overhanging cave that looks right on to the surf.

PRESLEY'S BAY ★★★ ■ 🏄

The beach here hosts some good peaks. However, you would only want to surf here if Lwandile, half an hour walk down the beach, is not working. The surf spot is just down from a small row of rustic holiday cottages, or 'camps' in the lingo of the Kei. The best time to surf is during a small swell early in the morning when it's glassy or light offshore. Accessible from the main road between Umtata and Port St Johns.

EBALOW ★★★★ ◆ 👑

Another great pointbreak, and a rare left-hander for the Eastern Cape. It needs a fair-sized swell, preferably a cyclonic easterly swell, or an outswinging frontal swell

PONDOLAND FEVER...PONDOLAND FEVER...PONDOLAND FEVER...POND

cliffs which dropped off hundreds of feet into the surging sea below. A solid ten foot swell was battering the base of the cliffs. Every time a wave broke there was a loud crack and the vibrations shook the earth as we walked. The spray from the in-cessant pounding hung over the cliffs like a shroud. At intervals of a few kilometres the path would wind inland and we'd know we were nearing a village when half-dressed children ambushed us, holding out both their hands and screaming, 'Sweets, sweets, sweets.'

Passing through the villages was like looking at pictures from 50 years ago. Women cut square blocks of earth from the ground to build rondavels. Men gathered in their Kraals listening to the tinny sounds of transistor radios.

No waves though, despite the fact that I had scrutinised every point and potential reef en–route. Like the true optimists that surfers are, I was convinced that where the cliffs ended I'd find a surfable wave.

By the time we did finally reach a beach, the light was fading quickly. Huge swells that comes in from the southeast. Best in light berg winds. Turn off from the Mpande road to the South, before hitting the coast. You will need a four-wheel drive but the scenery and surf will make it worth your while.

RAME HEAD ★★★ ◆ 〜

A long peninsula with a fast right point. This spot only works in big swell, when the other spots are out of control. It needs westerly winds, and is relatively protected from the stronger SW. It's a two-hour walk from Mpande along the beach.

SHARKS POINT ★★★★ ◆ 〜

This place gets some great waves, but is quite difficult to get to. In a bay sheltered by cliffs, the point is on the south side. Gets good when swell is in the 4–6' region, with light to moderate westerly winds. To get there, take a walk south from Mpande. It should take about half an hour.

MPANDE ★★★ ■ ⬠

This beachbreak provides some fun waves. There is a good lefthander that breaks into a channel near the rocks. Needs 2–4' easterly swells and light westerly winds. Also accessible from the Port St Johns / Umtata road. There is a campsite near the lagoon.

MNGAZI ★★★ ■ ⬠

A beachbreak in front of the river mouth goes off occasionally, when conditions are glassy and the swell is in the 2–5' region. It's signposted from the main road between Port St Johns and Umtata. Mngazi Bungalows Hotel is famous for its seafood dinners and sunny, relaxed atmosphere.

ND FEVER...PONDOLAND FEVER...PONDOLAND FEVER...PONDOLAND FE

straightened, peaked and crashed onto the beach, churning up tons of sand.

We collected drift-wood and lit a fire, ate a hastily prepared meal of instant soya and pasta, and dragged our fatigued bones into sleeping bags.

I fell asleep listening to the roar of the surf and gazing at the powdery arc sketched across the night sky by the Milky Way.

Nick was bitching about chlorinated water when I woke up, but there was a darting fire with breakfast simmering to redeem

him. The rain and wind of the previous day had disappeared during the night, and as the sun rose behind us, the beach turned to liquid gold and the pounding surf shimmered and glowed.

I peered down the beach into the murky white haze that hovered over the water, convinced I could see a pointbreak in the distance. Nick and James were still finishing the remnants of breakfast by the time I had my pack strapped on my back.

First, there was a river mouth to cross, a procedure which involved stuffing our

Port St Johns is a weird place. Spectacularly beautiful, with a dramatic geography, this frontier-like town is a whacky blend of wild African jungle, tribal culture and colonial town planning, with a faded, peeling facade and recent hippie culture thrown into the mix, so to speak.

Built on both sides of the mighty Umzimvubu River, which has sliced a steep gorge to the sea, forests carpet the earth and wild monkeys chatter in the undergrowth. There are several beaches hemmed in by a profusion of lush plants, birds and other wildlife, including the ferals who subsist in the bush.

The Mpondo people who live in the area call the river 'home of the hippopotamus'. Until the colonial trade in ivory and skins came to the area, the jungle and rivers teemed with wild animals, crocodiles and hippo.

However, those days belong in the history books. It retains a wild unkempt look. There are several backpacker lodges in the area and you are likely to come across some scraggly New Agers and ferals.

Several city slickers and former tourists have chilled out semi-permanently in Port St Johns, enjoying the 'minty' local crops and sometimes marrying into the local tribesfolk. One guy has become a sangoma (witchdoctor), and is fully kitted out in the regalia befitting his status.

There is no great surf, but it's a laid-back place that caters for travellers. There are a few waves at the Umzimvubu River mouth, depending on the sand banks. Keep an eye out for sharks. Second and Third beach, just to the south of the town, host a few waves now and then. Second Beach is more popular for surfing, and there are decent backpacker hotels around.

The atmosphere is tropical and relaxed. Both beaches are best in light offshore or glassy days. They pick up a lot of swell, but only work when it's small.

PONDOLAND FEVER...PONDOLAND FEVER...PONDOLAND FEVER...POND

backpack into a large, plastic survival bag, floating it on the water and swimming over to the other side. All done while hoping that there were no Great Whites, Hammerheads or Zambezis feeling peckish.

As the sun rose into the morning sky, the misty haze dissipated and I could see a rocky point probing the endless expanse of offshore, feathered, symmetrical blue lines that marched endlessly onto a yellow-white beach. My pace quickened. This had to be it.

As I neared, it became clear that this was a pointbreak of epic proportions. Dots of white stretched up the point at perfectly spaced intervals.

Waves from a distance are often deceitful, and lure one into false hope. Not this one. Focus came as fast as I could walk, but gradually I could see the lip, the wall, the spray off the back of the wave and the hollow sections. And then my heart dropped. Scrambling down the embankment 20 metres away was a surfer.

Three, four, five surfers in fact, and the dream of uncrowded perfection was shat-

Coffee Bay point, p. 135.

Kei pointbreak goes off at 8'.

MNTAFUFU *** ■ ⌷ ⌂

Offers a beachbreak with a right-hander that breaks off a reef on the south side. Works best on a small swell and westerly winds. This spot is at the end of the Lusikisiki road – you have to walk another 3 km south, to the mouth of the Mntafufu River, or catch a boat from further upstream.

MZIMPUNI *** ■ ⌂

A large bay with a right pointbreak at its southern end. This place needs a large southerly swell and morning offshore, or NW berg wind to work at its best. Some people walk to Mzimpuni from Mbotyi — about 4 km heading south. A 4x4 vehicle will get you there quicker.

MBOTYI **** ■ ⌷

A beautiful long beach dotted with A–frame peaks. At its best in a small to moderate east swell and light offshore NW winds. From Port St Johns, take the Lusikisiki road and follow the Mbotyi signs. As you approach the coast, the road gets steep and can be very slippery – impassable after heavy rains. This becomes an excellent excuse if you are on a surf trip during a holiday away from work! 'Sorry boss, we're trapped in Transkei. It's bad. Been raining here for weeks. The rivers have flooded and the roads are washed away. Looks like we'll be holed up here for at least another week.' Visitors can camp on the banks of the lagoon. It would be wise to have someone always at your camp, watching over your stuff. Some of the local guys will do it for free.

tered. The lone surfer had seen me too and we stared at each other like animals competing for the same carcass.

These guys looked like hardened surf seekers. In the background I made out a battered Land Rover and tents. Long, unkept beard, glazed eyes and gleaming custom shaped board, the first guy stood and waited for my arrival.

'Good waves,' I said, the international surfer's greeting. 'When the tide pushes,' he said, pointing at the monstrous lumps shifting across the horizon, 'that should wrap around the point. Then it will really be cooking.'

I thought it was cooking. I sat down on the rocks and watched Utopian waves wrap around the point, feather and scream down the line, tube sections throwing and peeling in pristine grandeur. The walls were steep, and they were grinding endlessly. And me with no surfboard.

But that changed in my mind. I was out there with my surfing buddies. Kev was racing down the line, going into a knee-popping, fin-ripping bottom turn that sent

To the North, the Wild Coast becomes sub-tropical.

ND FEVER...PONDOLAND FEVER...PONDOLAND FEVER...PONDOLAND FE

him into a rail grinding off-the-top. Ron was gunning through the sections of a feathering freight train and Fred was jamming verts all the way down the line.

We were all hooting. Sitting around the fire with Wiseman and the lads that Wednesday night I remembered a line from the film 'A River Runs Through It,' which cites the moments when all existence seems to fade.

It struck me that surfing is really about so many things, many of them infinitely indescribable.

It's about the endless dirt roads that stretch into a deep blue African sky, lonely farmhouses, reckless jols, and more than anything, it's about the changing patterns of the ocean and the gift of a perfect wave that comes along every few years and catches you in a fleeting moment of immortality.

I didn't need to be surfing that day, because I was. I could feel it. That's why, every day of my life, no matter how many thousands of miles away I am from the ocean, I'm a surfer.

KWAZULU-NATAL

Sub-tropical KwaZulu-Natal is sandwiched between the Indian Ocean to the east, the Drakensberg mountains to the west, tropical Mozambique to the north and the Transkei to the south.

Hot and humid in summer, warm and dryer in winter, Natalians live in a sub-tropical paradise. The surf is generally characterised by hollow beachbreaks and exposed reefs, best surfed in glassy, offshore conditions early or late in the day.

In winter, southern storm swells must travel further to influence this coast. While you get fewer winter swells than the Cape, the swell is often cleaner and more orderly.

In summer, the KwaZulu-Natal coast has surf almost every day, especially spots exposed to the ocean. There are four reasons for this. The continental shelf comes right up to the coast in parts, which means the deep ocean is nearby. Prevalent NE winds bring plenty of sloppy wind swell. Then there are fairly regular groundswells from the south. However, the big bonus is the prevalence of numerous cyclone swells in summer. Between November and April, tropical cyclones form off the east

coast of Madagascar. When they move south, they push in seriously big swell, often confined to the Mozambique and KwaZulu-Natal coast. A lot of spots are at their best in these easterly swells.

Generally, the best time to surf is early or late in the day, when prevailing NE or SW winds fade. During summer months, offshore days are rare due to the NE onshore wind, which is caused by high pressure cells in the Indian Ocean. These systems can create wind swell, depending on the duration and strength of the NE wind.

In winter, fronts pass closer to the area, and there are regular south swells, with SW to W offshore winds more common. Generally, the dawn patrol remains the best option for epic winter surf, as gentle NW land–breezes blow overnight and last until mid-morning. Many pointbreaks and protected reefs go off consistently in winter. Best time is February to July. The coast can be sharky, particularly on the rural north coast. The Natal Sharks Board (NSB) is efficient at maintaining shark nets at populated beaches.

KOSI BAY ** ■ ⌐ ⋈

The northern-most coastline of South Africa's eastern seaboard, almost on the border with Mozambique. The Kosi Bay area is an eco-tourism paradise. The protected Kosi Bay estuary is a pristine waterway, surrounded by lush marsh forest, mangrove, ferns and orchids. Crocs and hippos lurk in the Sihadhla River. Loggerhead turtles nest at nearby Bhang Nek, slightly to the south. There is surf potential further south. This coastline includes Dog Point, Black Rock, Island Rock, Hully Point and Gobey's Point. Explore.

SODWANA *** ■ ⌐ ⋈

This is a tropical diving and angling paradise. Large, lush coastal forests to explore. Stunning coastline. Good waves can be found on the beach in Sodwana Bay itself. Breaks left and right. Fickle banks, but can go off, breaking up to 6'. Good waves at Jesser Point, occasionally. Prevalent winds are onshore NE, but land breezes often blow at sunrise and sunset. Cyclone swell turns this coast on.

ST LUCIA ** ■ ⌐ ⋈

This spectacular 100 km stretch of coast runs beside an inland lake called Lake St Lucia. The mouth of this tropical estuary lies to the south, at St Lucia. Covered in a verdant mantle of jungle, this protected area comprises of several nature reserves. There are long beaches and the water is luke-warm, around 27° C. With the prevalent onshores, waves seem messy and all over the place, with most coral reefs near the shoreline. However, word has it that there are several world-class beachbreaks, and one or two reefs that go off in cyclone swells. Befriend a local, or go exploring on the beaches in the area. Otherwise, take a look at the point to the south of St Lucia at Mapelane.

ALKANTSTRAND **** ● ⌐

Sandbanks are held in place by the massive north breakwater, making Alkantstrand the best spot – certainly in terms of consistency – in the Richards Bay area. Wedging right-handers rebound off the 'dollose' and peel down the beach. As with most KZN spots, it's best in a SW wind. When the NE blows, you might like to check out 'Inside', a sheltered left-hander that breaks off the other side of the groyne. Amazingly, right on the edge of the shipping lane, inside the Richards Bay harbour itself, is the rare but excellent Señoritas, a bombora that comes to life in only the biggest cyclone swells.

MTUNZINI ** ■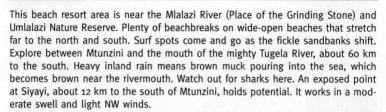

This beach resort area is near the Mlalazi River (Place of the Grinding Stone) and Umlalazi Nature Reserve. Plenty of beachbreaks on wide-open beaches that stretch far to the north and south. Surf spots come and go as the fickle sandbanks shift. Explore between Mtunzini and the mouth of the mighty Tugela River, about 60 km to the south. Heavy inland rain means brown muck pouring into the sea, which becomes brown near the rivermouth. Watch out for sharks here. An exposed point at Siyayi, about 12 km to the south of Mtunzini, holds potential. It works in a moderate swell and light NW winds.

ZINKWAZI **** ■

Travelling south of the Tugela River, you find this small resort near a reedy lagoon and narrow, rocky beach. It's 85 km from Durban. Some pretty good reef and sandbar options along the main beach. Consistent and fairly protected. A right-hander breaks off a headland to the south, mostly in winter. Needs solid SW swell and light westerly.

BLYTHEDALE * ●

Fickle beachbreaks and shifting sandbanks. But, as with many spots in KwaZulu-Natal, it can get classic. Doesn't handle over 5' and needs light westerly winds. A few good spots to the south, if you charm a local.

SALT ROCK ** ●

A left and right peak that breaks close to the beach. Popular with North Coast groms. It handles a 2–5' swell in light offshore winds (NW). Best time is early.

THOMPSONS BAY ** ■

Small, sheltered beach and a small streamlet. Starting to become a popular beach. Breaks fast and hard right on the beach due to shelving sandbanks. Lefts on a cyclone swell and fast right-handers off the tidal pool on a S swell. Low tide only.

SUNRISE ***** ◆

At the northern end of Ballito, lies this protected beach. A semi-point that enjoys excellent sandbar build-up in front of the rocks. The wave is faster than you expect, so positioning and the subtle art of the weave are the go. Right-handers only, unless you want to dive for crayfish. Fires on a small easterly swell and gentle offshores.

SURFERS ★★★ ■ ⬜

Just north of the main lifeguard hut at Ballito, a fast, hollow right-hander breaks off a large rock. Best at low tide in a SW swell with light offshore winds. Good from 2–6'. Needs the low tide, because, like most North Coast spots, it develops a deep inshore channel at high tide. On a big day, the rip can push you across the bay towards rocks on the other side. Can be a bit hectic. Lots of white water, closeouts and constant paddling.

BOG BAY ★★★ ♦ ⬜ ♛

A fickle spot that is highly sensitive to tides, wind and longshore drift. Big south swells scour away the sandbars and ruin this spot, while onshore winds and/or easterly swells push the banks back into place. Phenomenal at times, downright terrible at others. Low tide only.

SALMON BAY ★★ ■ ⬜ ♛

Something of a wildside, which means it's one of the last spots to get ruined by the NE. The bay is flanked on either side by left- and right-hand points.

TONGAAT ★★★ ■ ⬜

There are two exposed spots in the area, both with an aversion to wind. The point and beachbreak fire on a clean 3–5' groundswell. Produces a running, top to bottom barrel with the right conditions.

UMDLOTI ★★★★ ● ⬜

Built up, busy coastline. The beaches are exposed to the wind. Fickle, shifting banks make for a bit of a lucky dip sometimes. Best bet is the powerful, hollow right-hander on the south end of the town. The barrel is top to bottom. It handles up to 6'. Needs glassy conditions or light offshore winds. Best at 3–4'.

UMHLANGA ★★★ ● ⬜

A thriving, vibrant, upmarket beach resort area. Several surf options, including wedging beachbreaks and a few reefs, one of which is a big-wave spot. At the southern end, Cabana Beach (near the hotel) is the main spot. It's a left or right peak with the occasional high tide bowl. Bronze Beach offers a shifty peak. Best in small swell and light land breezes.

THE DURBAN PIERS

There was once a superlative spot in central Durban called the Bay of Plenty. Shaun Tomson learned his tube-riding skills there. It was famous as the home of the Gunston 500. Now called the Mr Price Pro, it remains the longest running professional surf event in history. In the late 1980's, the Bay began to lose its allure, and prominence, within the Durban surfing community.

There were two reasons for this. Firstly, three piers were built along the Durban beachfront – Bay Pier, New Pier and North Pier. As a result, the beachfront sandbanks were totally re-arranged, and the epic New Pier, North Beach and Dairy Bowl surf spots came into being.

Behind the development was a plan to reduce the effects of the longitudinal current that caused erosion along the beachfront, an obvious threat to the promenade's attraction as one of South Africa's busiest tourist venues.

Secondly, the hangout for the local beach community, Dante's Restaurant, was torn down in the early 1980's to make way for development. The clique moved away from the Bay and began to hang out at Dairy Beach between New Pier and North Pier. At the turn of the century, the hub shifted to the New Pier area, notably Bruce's Coffee Shop.

The construction of the piers may have resulted in the irrevocable overhaul of Durban's surf spots, but North Beach and New Pier now offer some of the most powerful sandbank waves around. Both handle solid westerly storm swells and big tropical cyclone swells. When the big easterly swells arrive, the Dairy Bowl turns on. The sand gets into the beachfront through wave action or from sand pumped up by the dredging of the harbour mouth. Dredgers are located at Addington Beach, Dairy Beach and Bay of Plenty.

'Surf city' has the largest population of surfers in the country. Peppered with surf shops and spots, it's an ideal city surfing locale. There are lots of spots, from mellow beachbreaks to grindingly hollow reef and beachbreaks. The nightlife hums. The beach culture is a powerful force along the promenade, with the bronzed surf crew hanging out at trendy hangouts bedecked in the latest, slick fashions.

In terms of the surf, the Bluff, a large headland at the south end of the harbour, blocks off the swell from the beachfront. If a 6' south swell is running, then the spots along the southern Bluff will be firing but New Pier might only be 3'. Spots in the southern corner of the beachfront – such as Vetch's Reef and Addington – are often flat. South swells refract around the Bluff, and begin breaking only from South Beach. The waves get bigger as you head north, past the Wedge, Dairy Pier (New Pier), North Pier, Bay Pier and Snake Park.

When easterly swells pull through, the Durban basin fills up with swell, turning on spots like the Dairy Bowl, a famously powerful sandbar wedge between North Pier and New Pier.

COUNTRY CLUB ** ● ⌂

Formally known as African Beach, this beachbreak used to be a blacks-only beach during the apartheid days. It's in front of the fancy Durban Country Club. It's sensitive to the tides and breaks left or right. Goes off at times, when the sand is in the right place. Offers an excellent shorebreak.

BATTERY BEACH ** ● ⌂

This beachbreak can be found at the northern end of Durban's beachfront in front of the Natal Command army base. It gets incredibly powerful at times. When the swell is 3–4' at New Pier, Battery can be a solid 6'. Like all the northern beaches, surf here on low tide for the outer banks, and high tide for the shorebreaks.

SNAKE PARK *** ■ ⌂

Yes, this break is near the Durban Snake Park. The utility wave at the Park is the midbreak wave that peels off the shotgun pier. Further down the beach in front of the wire-frame lighthouse is a dual direction peak that gets good. Unfortunately this peak isn't always there: the fickle nature of sand means that the bank regularly builds up and gets washed away. In the old days, Snake Park used to have a reputation of being a hardcore locals-only spot, with many outbursts or aggression along the beachfront. However, over the years, the old crew have dissipated or moved on to other parts of the beachfront. The venom of the orginal Snake Park crew is now a thing of the past.

Bay of Plenty ★★★ ● ⌐

Once the HQ of surfing in South Africa. The replacement of the solid Patterson groins with the pylon piers (allowing for long-shore drift) probably ruined one of the best man-made waves in Southern Africa. What remains of this once perfect beachbreak is still a reasonably consistent wave which peels right on the outside with the occasional left bowl at higher tides. Although not in the same category as North Beach or New Pier, it's the least crowded of the pier waves in Durban, and probably first of the town's spots to register a sweeping ground swell. On the downside, there are only a few days a year when the wave will link right through. Even for those who know the ins and outs of negotiating the Bay, the lack of linkage can get frustrating.

North Beach ★★★★★ ■ ⌐

An incredibly good wave when it's on. North Beach is now more consistent than Bay of Plenty and is home to a zillion bodyboarders. A crunching right-hander that barrels its way across a sandbank. Handles up to 10' and has been the scene of some epic barrel riding feats. On the lower tide, stick to the strong-shouldered right that comes off the pier, as these seldom close out or run fat. Anything from 1–10' looks good. A pushing tide brings the action closer in with a walling, left-hand bowl that pushes towards the pier. Best conditions are a solid swell and a light westerly breeze. If you're a hardboard surfer, surf only when the blackball is up, and stay away from the bathing area.

Dairy / New Pier ★★★★★ ■ ⌐

Possibly the most popular 200 metres of aquatic real estate in South Africa. On the north side of the beach is the Dairy Bowl, a slow V-shaped peak that works best on a very deep tide and during an onshore. However the real diamonds of Dairy are the lefts that break during clean east swells. On the opposite end of the beach, is New Pier, Durban's surf central. Ironically the new concrete piers that ruined the once famous Bay of Plenty, simultaneously created this spitting right-hander. Every bit a world class beachbreak. At low tide in a lined up swell with SW winds, this wave peels from directly in front of the pier head and winds all the way down to Dairy. It has been ridden well over 10', made possible by jumping off the end of the pier during breaks in the sets. At its best it is incredibly fast and very hollow, straight from takeoff, but what it provides day in and day out is a consistent hot dog wave for the hordes of locals who call it home.

Wedge ★★★ ■ ⌐

Just in front of the beachfront promenade and south of the New Pier. A beachbreak that offers respite from the crowds. Best on a broken swell and lower tide.

SOUTH BEACH / ADDINGTON ★★★ ● ⊏⊐

These two fairly consistent spots lie to the south of the Wedge. They are usually smaller than the spots to the north. Both beaches are ideally angled to handle the south westerlies, which blow straight offshore here. Best on the low tide. Occasionally, good waves can be had, depending on the sandbanks. User-friendly waves for less experienced surfers.

VETCH'S REEF ★★★★ ◆

Located half a kilometre out to sea, Vetch's Reef is actually the remnants of a failed breakwater from the turn of the 19th century. The reef, originally built to enclose a yacht mole, is perfectly angled to produce the longest rights in the Durban area, but needs a rare combination of north swells and west winds for it to work. Best during the summer to autumn months, when these are most likely. It has two distinct peaks, the outside 'Block' and the inside 'Urchins' reef, which will link together to form one long ride on the biggest swells. Watch out here. Vetch's is ridiculously fast and sucky, and deceptively dangerous. The Block in particular has a long list of victims. Strictly high tide entry only. Beware the stonefish waiting on what remains of the old breakwater.

ANSTEYS ★★★★★ ■ ⊏⊐

On Durban's Bluff, a less populated residential area. The attraction of the Bluff is that it can handle a wind swinging to northeast, and will stay smooth for several hours longer than town. Ansteys is the utility wave in the area, and is more user-friendly than elsewhere on the Bluff. Mostly it's a zippy right-hander over a nicely tapered sandbar, but you can scoop some very good lefts if you're the gambling type. Best when a moderate swell is running, particularly if it is from the east. The

SEPIA MOMENTS FROM SOUTH BEACH
By Tony Heard

The thing about surfing is not that it is a sport. It is a lifestyle – of fun, danger and individualism. It is about waves and about people, in that order, not about teams.

It has produced its own music, culture, films, poetry, food, outlook, cranks and greats. It is, with the microchip, one of the revolutionary features of our age. Even the mighty Internet pays it a compliment — surfing the Net.

I dare to suggest that no generation of youth has had its lifestyle so vastly influenced by a physical activity. Upper middle-class men and women have stowed their neat suits and tidy jobs and dropped out of the rat race to take up the ultimate nirvana trip that is the surf life, sometimes permanently.

With surfing, you can evade the rigours of urban gridlock without, as many sports

Cave Rock, p. 154.

Tongaat, p. 148.

bigger the swell the further out the wave peaks on a sand covered reef that sticks like a finger straight out to sea. It has been ridden over 15' and at a good size presents an exciting and makeable alternative to Cave Rock although the paddle out is testing.

CAVE ROCK ★★★★★ ◆ 👑

Awesome! It's the only way to describe this pit–bulled reef monster. Arguably the best barreling wave in Durban, if not Natal, Cave Rock breaks round and hard. It throws out an insane, top-to-bottom tube. In glassy conditions, you're talking superlative. For epic conditions, a clean south swell is needed, with requisite light offshore. The swell can be big, up to 10–15', but needs to be spaced evenly and cleanly. Gets dangerously shallow during the low tide. The paddle out can be very hairy when its going off its face. Stay away if you don't have your balls with you.

BRIGHTON ★★★ ■ ⬭ 👑

Brighton, like Ansteys, offers more variety than the Rock. On the right swell, the lefts that whistle off the pool are awesome, although slightly sectiony. Watch out for the bricks here. You're surfing over a minefield of rocks. The middle peak is the most popular, with plenty blow–outs when the surf hits the four foot and over mark. When it tops 8', the paddle here scores high on the Ouch-o-meter.

Further down the beach is Pigs Reef, which is your classic underwater point. Best during morning land breezes. It's not as sensitive to swell direction and tide changes as the Rock, so you don't need to wait for the perfect tide and sweeping southerly swell.

people do, ending up in equally oppressive forms of team discipline.

Those other sports, which shall remain nameless for fear of instant knee-capping or worse, can be healthy, even satisfying, and wow the captivated fans, but are no intellectual escape from the controlled lives we live in. Just look at the boring team rituals required in so many sports, and the equally boring, Messianic sense of commitment to win.

Few sports can provide the individual escape of surfing, though skiing gets close. But give me a monster wave over a mogul any day. Surfing gets right into your head, in a liberating way.

The constant change in the mood of the sea gives surfing an unpredictability that is unique (and I know journalists should not use 'unique' more than a maximum of five times in a lifetime).

Before the short board, in the 1940s to 1960's, every board, whether the large Olo type or 15-foot guns traceable respectively

REUNION

Works in the northeasterly onshore. Situated on the south side of the Bluff, the onshore wind channels around the Bluff and blows offshore / sideshore here. It can handle this, as long as the wind isn't too strong. Doesn't like big swell.

....SOUTH COAST

AMANZIMTOTI

Where a concrete jungle mixes with a luxuriant real jungle. This straight strip of coastline offers rideable waves all the way along, as well as the occasional reef. Inyoni Rocks and Toti Pipe are both popular. Best early in the morning, during light offshores and moderate swells. Just for the record, the Inyoni Rocks to Winkelspruit stretch once had the unfortunate distinction of having the most recorded shark attacks in the world. However, the majority of these occurred before shark nets were put in place in 1962.

WARNER BEACH ***

Home of the South Coast surf underground! On any given day at Warner Beach there is usually an army of good surfers out in the water, ripping the waves apart with trademark aggression. Interesting high tide shorebreaks to ease the summer doldrums, particularly at Baggies, which handles winds from both the SW and the NE. To the north of Baggies is Pulpit, a semi-pointbreak that needs a fair bit of swell before it starts to work.

to Hawaii or Aussie – was beach-bound, a solemn totem pole, like something found on Easter Island.

It was immobile out of the surf. It had to be locked up and chained like a Great Dane, standing tall against beach buildings – though it would take a furniture truck to steal.

The long board, moreover, was rather masculine-orientated, not easily used solo by less robust women, though the 'wahines' of Hawaii showed the way to wave feminism and assertiveness ages ago. 'Wahines' even dropped in on kings.

Some women of my early surf years on Durban's South Beach, like Vera Salzman could handle a 'gun'. Wendy Hall would ride two–up with adept, angular surfer Bruce Giles – and even stand on her head while white water foamed all around. And this was achieved without leash, skeg or shark nets.

But the short, light surfboard made for easier moves, in the curl or on the land.

GREEN POINT ★★★★★ ◆ ▱

Another of the many pointbreaks on the KZN south coast. Epic wall breaks on a sandy bottom. This spot offers long hollow waves with the right swell direction.

SCOTTBURGH POINT ★★★★ ■ ▱

The wave off the swimming pool at Scottburgh is a typical KZN south coast, sand bottom, right pointbreak which can get very good if the banks are right. Can get ruined when the river comes down in flood and cuts deep holes through the banks. Scotties handles strong SW winds and a southerly swell up to 10'. There is fierce localism around though, so make sure you show some respect.

KELSO / HAPPY WANDERERS ★★★★ ■ ▱

A right pointbreak with long rides. More of a rolling wave than a genuine top to bottom barrel. Peels for well over 300 metres at times. Breaks from 3–8'. There are a few other quality waves in the area. Locals are fiercely protective, but hang around long enough, and you might be admitted to the inner circle.

THE SPOT ★★★★★ ■ ▱ ♛

In a rural area at a place called Mfazazana/Sipofo. You used to have to pay off a local chief, or one of his representatives to be able to park and surf here. There are no nets, so it can be a tad sharky. But well worth the risk, with great walls and a barrelling inside section. Likes offshores or light SW. One of the longest rides around.

SEPIA MOMENTS...SEPIA MOMENTS...SEPIA MOMENTS...SEPI

It could be taken anywhere, used by anyone who had some balance and was prepared to face whatever swells Davey Jones' Locker had to offer (as we used to sing when body-surfing, to keep courage up while waiting for 'backies' or 'slides' in days before the nets – the days when Glenwood High's Clive Dumane was taken off Addington beach).

In fact, our main source of revenue – apart from assiduously spotting rolling 'tom', silver coins, washed by high tide shorebreaks up the beach – was laying shark bait for the fishermen from South Pier.

This entailed gripping said bait, complete with huge hook in it, between the ankles and paddling vast distances to the shark territory, gingerly dropping it for the sharks to swallow, and paddling like hell back to the Pier, where friends collected one shilling a trip, enough, soon, to make a new plywood or masonite board.

Putting surfing on the move, with short

KZN South Coast

Scottburgh Point, p. 156.

UMZUMBE ★★★★ ■ ⌂

South of Hibberdene, Umzumbe is a right sand–bottomed pointbreak with two distinct sections. When they link up, on lined-up SW swells, they can produce very long rides. Umzumbe has a strong local crew because it is consistent and holds moderate SW winds.

BANANA BEACH ★★★★ ■ ⌂

The next spot south of Umzumbe, another right sand-bottomed pointbreak that peels off an outcropping of rocks and can, on good days, get very hollow. It will begin to close out over 8' and is vulnerable to side-shore winds.

SUNWICH PORT ★★★★ ◆ ⌂ ⌂

About 5 minutes drive south of Banana Beach, turn into a small carpark directly off the South Coast road near a large Avis sign. A fickle right reef that needs a solid swell. Super–hollow wave over shallow reef. These half water, half sand barrels are best on an outgoing tide in a SW swell 3–6'.

ST MIKES ★★★★★ ◆ ⌂ ⌂

In a seaside resort town called St Michaels-on-Sea, this grinding right-hander cooks. It's also pretty consistent. St Mikes has elements of reef, pointbreak and sandbar rolled into one. The swell hits the corner of a tidal pool and jacks up into a long wall that screams on to the beach. Gets really good. Water can be murky. The down side is that it is very popular, and therefore usually crowded. Inexperienced people will not be able to get many waves.

boards, was at the root of the Surf Revolution. Surfers from Malibu or Waikiki or Jersey would find themselves with their own custom-made boards at Jeffrey's Bay.

My journalist brother Ray freighted his surfboard aboard Air Force One when US President Johnson went, with the White House Press Corps, for a meeting of his Vietnam allies in Hawaii. Ray would loudly and successfully berate commercial airlines when they

took golf clubs, but tried to refuse surfboards.

The days of big boards were very different to the equipment you get these days. The only case I know of where a board was liberated from South Beach was when Cliffie Honeysett innovatively shipped his massive, banana-shaped board from Durban by coaster in 1956, and managed to deliver it to me in Camps Bay.

It was the time when John Whitmore was pioneering the surf industry in Cape

MARGATE ★★★

A long stretch of beach with multiple shifty peaks. Although, in front of the point, a small, shallow reef provides for some quick, hollow takeoffs. Best up to 4–6' with light westerlies and a low tide.

LUCIEN ★★★★

This is the best summer spot on the south coast. A left-hand pointbreak sheltering a beachbreak from those summer northeasterlies. Best on the high tide for a grinding shorebreak.

SOUTHBROOM ★★★★

Excellent sand-bottomed rights break off a large, round, rock-fringed grassy hill. Very popular with travelling surfers because it's easy to find and parking is easy.

TRAFALGAR ★★★

Average to good beachbreak and deepwater right-hand reef. One of the few south coast spots that cooks on a big swell, if you make the paddle through the beachbreak. Also holds moderate SW winds. Very quiet spot.

TO STRAND ★★★★

Just north of Port Edward, you will find this spot where rights break off a small grassy headland. Can get very hollow depending on the tide. One of the better big wave breaks on the South Coast.

Town, in between handling the Glen beachbreaks which, through sheer turbulence, produced such outstanding surfers as the Paarmans, Meneseses and Strongs.

Once the revolution took off, there was nothing that could stop it. The women surfers made up for lost ground, doing their own affirmative action by standing up, with people like world-class Sally Sturrock blossoming.

Black surfers, historically concentrated on certain remote beaches by South Africa's idiotic race laws, began – around the time of Steve Biko – to break out and to be seen prominently hanging ten, locked in and hitting the lip all over the place, including the pristine, safer, once whites-only beaches.

It was all aboard, literally, for the cult of the millennium.

John Whittle, New Pier.

SA SEASONS

Summer – November to February
Autumn – March to April
Winter – May to August
Spring – September to October

WHAT SURFBOARDS DO I NEED?

South Africa has every conceivable permutation in the setup of its surf spots. There is sand. There are rocks. There are beachbreaks. There are pointbreaks. There are rivermouths, piers, groynes, dollose (protective concrete barriers), sandbanks and shipwrecks. There are reef-point-beach-break combinations. Some waves break fast and hard; others are mushy and weak. Some waves offer long, winding walls that grind down a reef like a freight train. Then there are those that rear up and spit like an African cobra. Try to bring at least two boards to cover the conditions you are likely to encounter. Bring a slightly wider and shorter board (6'4" to 6'8") for average 3–6' beachbreak or reef waves. For the big days, make sure you are not undergunned. Get a slightly narrower, down-the-line 6'10" (or bigger) for riding big waves. The main purpose for this board should be for solid 6–8' pointbreak days, when you want to draw speed lines along a feathering wall. To save costs and travel hassle, pre-order your boards from a South African shaper, or surf shop, and pick them up when you arrive.

WHAT WETSUITS DO I NEED?

Play it safe and bring all your wetsuits. The South African coast has a number of seasonal and climatic variations. Temperatures vary depending on the currents and winds. The only time board shorts are a sure bet is peak summer in the Indian Ocean along the East Coast, from East London to KwaZulu-Natal. If your stay falls anywhere between November and March, board shorts will suffice, but bring a lycra chafe vest or spring suit in case. If you plan to travel around, especially further south, bring it all! That means chafe vest, booties, 4x3 fullsuit steamer AND spring suit. For instance, a spring suit, or even board shorts, might be good enough for East London on a sunny day in April, but the wind might switch, and the temperature plummet, when booties and a full suit is required. This is particularly true for the Atlantic side of the Cape Peninsula and West Coast. In fact, it holds true more for summer than winter. This is because the summer southeast trade winds create an effect called upwelling. The strong offshore winds push the top layer of the sea away from the land, pulling colder water up from the depths. However, as autumn arrives (April) the southeaster dies down and the water warms up. During bergwind conditions, you could be surfing in balmy 18-degree water a week after it was a frigid 11 degrees! On the Indian Ocean side of the peninsula, it's warmer in summer, but colder in winter. The further north you go up the east coast, the warmer the water gets. During summer the Indian Ocean is often warm enough for baggies, but sometimes the NE onshore brings cold water in, and you need a spring suit. It all depends.

WHAT IS THE BEST TIME OF YEAR?

There are waves all over South Africa all around the year. Spring and autumn get classic. Winter is awesome. Summer is less consistent, but gets good, especially in KwaZulu-Natal. For grinding winter conditions, surf between May and September. Peak surfing season is June to August, when popular spots are the most crowded. The mildest months are in autumn

In summer, you need a full wetsuit at the Hoek, which is near Cape Town.

(March-May) and spring (September-October). Summer and winter bring extremes in heat and flat seas or huge seas and bad weather, respectively. In autumn, the weather is warm, but not sweltering, and the first sign of winter arrives with big, clean frontal swells. The West Coast gets good at this time. There are many calm days, and clean, big groundswells pushing up from the south.

In spring, there are late winter swells and frontal storms to keep up the stoke. It's not quite as consistent as peak winter, but the advantage is that the big cold fronts, huge swell and nasty weather are more infrequent. Less crowds too. During winter, there is surf almost every day for up to a week at a time, sometimes longer. Sometimes it's out-of-control and too big for many of the spots. In summer, it's often onshore in the Eastern Cape and KwaZulu-Natal, but there is plenty of fun, mushy wind swell to wile away sun-kissed days. Every now and then, a big cyclone swell hits the East Coast. Offshore winds are less frequent, but

there are spots that work in the prevalent NE onshore wind.

HOW DOES ONE GET AROUND?

The best way for surfers to travel around South Africa is by car. Get a group of people together and hire one. It's affordable, and makes it easier to find waves. Many good spots are in rural areas, and are difficult to access.

WHAT ABOUT CRIME?

Like sharks, one has to take certain precautions to prevent attack. In the city, follow global guidelines that you would for, say, Rio de Janeiro. Obvious precautions reduce the risk. Don't be ostentatious. Most beaches are safe but always lock your vehicle. Put valuables away under the seats or locked in the trunk. Put you car keys in your wetsuit pouch or find a hiding place under a rock, away from possible prying eyes. Don't leave your surfboards on the roof, pack them in the car. Melted wax is a small price to pay for a safe board.

IS THERE HEAVY LOCALISM?

Sometimes. But it's nowhere near the heavy vibe you can get in Hawaii or parts of California, and now, even Australia. Urban growth has led to crowded conditions at city spots, and occasionally at big-name spots out of town. Like a canine marking territory, some spots do have the occasional aggro local. Traditionally, you get flareups at places like Glen Beach, Llandudno, Scottburgh and Supertubes in J–Bay. In the winter season, Supertubes gets insanely crowded, with up to 100 surfers scratching around in the lineup. It can be a bunfight, with frequent outbursts of aggression. Disrespect from visitors has prompted local groups to act as 'guardians' of the break.

Sometimes accused of being vigilantes who abuse the new system, the situation does seem to have improved. Other places, like Llandudno, have had generations of locals with abusive personalities that pick on grommets and people they don't know. However, most of the time, even at the populated beaches, you just need to bide your time, act friendly, be polite and wait your turn. If someone threatens you, ignore them. To lessen the chance of crowds, surf early or late in the day. The alternative is to find quiet, lesser-known rural spots, or surf well-known spots on either side of the winter surfing season between May and the end of August.

USEFUL WEB RESOURCES

Main tourism portals
travel.iafrica.com : Travel portal
www.tourism.co.za : Travel resource
www.satour.org : SA Tourism Agency portal
www.places.co.za : Travel directory

Regional tourism portals
www.kapstadt.de : About Cape Town
www.cape-town.org : Cape Town Tourism site
www.gardenroute.co.za : Southern Cape
www.durbanet.co.za : About Durban
www.kzn.org.za : KwaZulu-Natal Tourism
www.ectourism.co.za : Eastern Cape Tourism

General
www.robinauld.co.za : Surfing bard
www.sonsurf.co.za : Christian surfing
www.jbu.co.za : Jeffrey's Bay Underground
www.shark.co.za : Natal Sharks Board
www.ccii.co.za : Coastal weather data
www.saws.co.za : SA Weather Services
www.5fm.co.za : Music and clubbing guide
www.eatingout.co.za : Restaurant guide
www.aardvark.co.za : Search for SA stuff

Surfing portal
www.wavescape.co.za

Media
www.zigzag.co.za | www.blunt.co.za
www.sa-bodyboarding.co.za

Nature and adventure sports
www.ecoafrica.com
www.adventure-village.co.za

Car hire
www.hertz.co.za | www.budget.co.za
www.avis.co.za | www.tempestcarhire.co.za

Accommodation
www.btsa.co.za | www.backpackers.co.za
www.backpack.co.za | www.safarinow.com

Shapers
www.geraghtyshapes.co.za
www.lazyb.co.za | www.biltsurf.com
www.sequencesurf.com/shapers
www.wavescape.co.za/bitch.htm

South African slang is a mixture of languages and cultures. There are influences from the Cape Malay and indigenous peoples, notably the Xhosa, Zulu and Sotho. European and Eastern settlers have also arrived on our shores over the centuries, and have helped create a linguistically disparate melting pot. Surfers, with their unique style of speaking, have borrowed from this great semantic source and mixed in surf terms to create a dynamic dictionary.

DISCLAIMER: This list contains words that some people may find offensive. If you are of fragile temperament, stop here. The words listed below are taken from a variety of sources, some of which do not necessarily represent the South African surfing culture of today.

KEY: Pronunciation in single quotes next to the word. Meanings below. The symbol * denotes the Germanic 'g' sound, as if about to spit.

AG A multi-purpose word, pronounced like the 'ach' in German. 'Ag, no man' (sign of irritation). Can precede any sentence for various effects, such as the more neutral, 'Ag, I don't know.' Used by some people as a stand-alone expletive.

AGGRO Aggressive. Someone who brings bad karma into the water.

AMPED Full of energy. Usually induced by adrenalin, feeling wired or high on fear, either before paddling into a huge ocean.

AS WELL (Accent on 'as') Also, me too. A person who says, 'Jees, I'm kished bru.' (Gee, I'm tired bro) might get this reply, 'Ja, I am as well.'

AXED Crushed, wiped out or whacked.

AWESOME Incredible. Used as another word for the sheer quality and size of a wave. 'That wave at Supers was awesome, man!'

AITA! ('Ay–tah') Greeting. 'Aita brah!' Originated in the townships among the youth, and is still used.

BABALAS ('Bub–ba–lars') The hangover from hell, fondly referred to as a 'barbie'.

BABE Sexist term for a woman.

BACKSTOP The little wad of tobacco and dagga pips between the gerrick and the dagga in a bottleneck.

BAFF Fart.

BAGGIES We don't call them board shorts or Bermudas or other naffy names. They are baggies. You wear them when the water is lekker warm.

BAKKIE ('Buk-ky') Pickup truck (US) 'Ute' (Australia).

BALLIE Old man

BANE Marijuana. 'Let's make a bane.'

BANKIE Bank packet. Common receptacle for a dagga stash.

BARNIE Fight, punchup.

BARREL Tube. When you get tubed on a wave, you ride the barrel. You do this by 'pulling in' and 'getting slotted'.

BEFOK, BEFUCK Wild, crazy, excellent. This is used two ways. 'He went befok.' (He lost his cool, threw his toys out of the cot, went ballistic or totally crazy) or 'That's befuck!' (That's great!)

BERGIE A hobo who hangs out on the streets of Cape Town. The term Bergie originates from the Berg (Mountain).

BILTONG Jerky (US). This is specially prepared dried raw meat, made from beef, venison or ostrich. Good biltong is manna to your average full-bodied 'Surfrikans'.

BLEAK Disappointed, sad. 'Since Sarah axed Rick, the oke's been lank bleak.'

BLIKSEM Hit, punch. 'I'm going to bliksem that doos!' (I am going to hit that c**t.)

BLOTTO Extremely inebriated.

BOATMAN Waveski rider. Affectionate term for someone who rides a paddle ski. *See* goatboat and windmill.

BODYBOARDER Surfers who rides waves lying down on a spongelike board. *See* doormat, sponge, gutslider, speedbump. To their credit, bodyboarders usually rise above these insults.

BOER Afrikaans farmer.

BOERE Slightly used word that refers to the police. Especially poignant in the dark days of apartheid.

BOEREWORS Farmstyle sausage. (Literally, 'farmer's sausage'). It is a spicy sausage made from hundreds of secret recipes. It is consumed in vast quantities on braais all over the country.

BOK Keen. 'Bok for the jol' (Keen to party.)

BOOGER Bodyboarder. *See* doormat, sponge, gutslider, speedbump.

BOS Bush. But also crazy, named after South African soldiers who were psychologically damaged in the Angolan war. 'Going bos or bossies' Going totally whacko, going bush crazy, doing something extreme.

BOTTLENECK The broken-off neck of a bottle. This becomes the perfect orifice for making a lung-wrenching dagga pipe.

BRAAI Barbecue (US) or Barbie (Aus). Probably the biggest semantic gift given to the world by South Africa. You make a braai with wood in a metal drum or between bricks. You cook your boerewors, lamb chops and sosaties on it. With your meal you eat mielie pap, salads, rolls and other stuff. You drink a Castle beer, or maybe a 'spook and diesel'. Sometimes, if you have caught some kreef, you will have a fish braai.

BRAH Surf brother, associate, peer. In fact, anyone on this planet, including women.

BROER ('Broo') Brother, friend. A variation of brah. Variations in tone emanate from all over South Africa. It is now spelt Bru by most SA surfers. In the Eastern Cape, a semantic hotbed of slang, it's often pro-

nounced 'brorr' or 'braaah', with a longer vowel sound. Also bru, brah, bror, bro.

BRU *See* above.

BUNNY CHOW Indian or Malay curry inside a hollowed out loaf of white bread. Surfers from Durban grew up on this food. Best when the bread is fresh.

BUST When you get caught. Another meaning is to 'bust' a pipe, or be the person who lights the pipe.

BUTTON Mandrax pill. A nasty pill from the East that people crush into powder and mix in with their bottleneck pipes.

CAPE DOCTOR The Southeaster howls across the Cape Peninsula in summer, often forming a whispy white cloud that rolls over Table Mountain in the shape of a 'table cloth'.

CARVING When a hottie slices up a wave using his board as a carving knife. Another term for high-performance surfing.

CHARF Tease or make fun.

COOLIE A cooldrink.

CHECK Look, do you see? 'You check' (See what I mean? Do you follow? (Are you with me?) or 'Check this out' (Look at this) or 'Are you checking me skeef?' (Are you looking at me crooked, in other words, do you want to fight me?)

CHINA A friend, colleague or acquaintance, or someone you don't know at all. It can be used aggressively. 'Are you tuning me kak, China?' (Are you giving me shit, mate?)

CHIPS ('Chups') 'Look out!' A warning. Someone will yell it just before the lip at Cave Rock renders you senseless, the bouncer's fist greets your jaw or the 'boere come and bust you for smoking dagga' (the cops catch you smoking dope).

CHORB A charming teenage term for a pimple or zit.

CHUCK Depart, leave, go, split.

CLASSIC Excellent, perfect, incredible. This is one of many superlatives in SA surf lingo. It denotes the best extreme achieved. 'The waves are classic.' or 'That boy / girl is classic.' or 'I had a classic time.

CLOSEOUT When the wave breaks at the same time all the way down the line.

COOKING Good surf. Nothing to do with preparing food. When the surf is cooking, then it's 'going off its face', it's 'firing' or it's 'pumping'. In other words, the surf is big, clean, has excellent shape and there are plenty of waves in a set. If someone 'cooks', they are good at surfing.

COOL The universal word referring to all things hip, okay, good, nice, funky, classic and kief. The latest variation of this famous word is kewl, pronounced koo–el, which comes from Internet chat groups.

CRANKING Good surf. *Also* firing, smoking, going ballistic, going off, cooking, off its face, classic, kraaking, pumping.

CRASH Go to sleep. 'Do you want to crash out at my porsie?' (Do you want sleep over at my place?)

CRIPPLE A kneeboarder.

DAGGA ('Dag–gah') Dope, marijuana.

DECK Flatten, punch. 'I decked him after he dropped in on my wave.'

DIP Punch. 'I dipped him after he slept with my girfriend.'

DOF ('Dorf') Stupid. Someone who is dof, is not necessarily that way all the time. It is often used to describe a temporary loss of brain cells. 'Don't be dof, you stupid doos.'

DOOBIE Dope, joint, spliff.

DOORMAT Bodyboarder. *See* shark biscuit, sponge, gutslider, speedbump. Derogatory, but vaguely descriptive, term for bodyboarders, who dislike 'boogie boarder' more, for some reason. In Oz, there are a number of interesting variations, such as Esky lid (cool box lid) and toilet lid.

DOOS Female genitalia. 'You are such a doos.' This means you are a complete idiot.

DOP Booze, or to fail school. 'One dop too many' (One drink too many). The other meaning of dop is when someone says, 'I dopped school.'

DORK Pimple or a feeble person.

DORP Small town. Don't be confused when

someone says, 'Let's go for a dop in that dorp.'

DOS Sleep.

DRILLED Axed, dumped, wiped-out.

DIK ('Duk') Thick, beefy, big, full. A person can be dik or you can get dik after a big meal. 'That rugby player is lank dik' (That rugby player is especially big).

DOOB Joint. *See* joint, spleef, number, etc.

DROP IN When another surfer takes off in front of you on a wave.

DUBUS Big, huge.

DUCKDIVE To duck under a broken wave by pushing the front of your surfboard under the water, then levering the back of the board with your knee or foot as the wave passes overhead. The desired result is to pop out the back perfectly, and then smirk when you realise the guy next to you has been washed back 15 metres.

DUMP A closeout wave dumps you.

DUMPY Smallish brown beer bottle. You drink your dop out of a dumpy.

DURBAN POISON A type of dagga.

DURBS Durban.

DWAAL ('Dwarl') Dreamlike state. This word describes that vacuous, blank state a person gets into sometimes, especially after sleep deprivation. 'I have been in a dwaal today after downing that half-jack of whisky last night.'

EINA ('Aynah') Ouch. Widely used. Derived from Afrikaans. You can shout 'Eina!' in sympathy when a shark haps (bites) your buddies' buttocks while surfing in the Kei.

EK SE ('Ek sair') I tell you. An affirmative phrase to add impact to what you are communicating. Used in a fascinating variety of contexts all over the country. 'Let's hit the jol, ek se.'

FADE Lose strength, or power. When you back out of something, you fade. But a wave fades on the inside if the water gets deeper.

FIREMAN The fireman is the second to pull on the dope pipe. The fireman lights two matches held together and holds it to the pipe for the person 'busting' it. The fireman gets the next hit.

FIRING Cooking surf. Another superlative to describe good surf. 'Hey brah, Super's is firing on all cylinders, ek se.'

FUDGE PACKER Graphic description of someone engaging in anal sex.

FULL ON Absolutely, right on, to the limit. This is a definite affirmation or agreement, or trying to express an act that goes right to the edge. It could be used in this context: 'That was a full-on drop-in.' (That was definitely a drop-in.)

FULLY This is also an affirmation. If this was the question: 'Did you check Occy pull off that insane move at Boneyards?' this might be the answer: 'Fully bru.'   -

GAFFED Stoned. 'Shew bru, that joint made me so-o-o gaffed ek se.'

GATSTAD ('G*ut–stut') Grahamstown. Gat means hole in Afrikaans, stad means town.

GATVOL ('G*at–fawl') Fed up. 'He was gatvol of the crowds at J-Bay.'

GERBE ('G*air–b–ear') Shark.

GERRICK A piece of silver foil from a cigarette box, or the cardboard from the box, that is laid out square, rolled up and bent into a circle. This is then placed in the bottom of the bottleneck so the dagga doesn't fall out when taking a hit.

GESUIP ('G*esayp') Drunk.

GIF ('G*erf') Not a computer image. This is the more sleazy version of kief.

GLASSY When the texture of the ocean is like glass. Smooth conditions because there is no wind.

GOATBOAT A derogatory term for a paddle skier, the sort of person that goes out in the surf paddling on a canoe that looks like a half-sucked lozenge. The reason why standup surfers don't like them much is because goatboats paddle faster. If in the wrong hands, they can also wreak havoc in the water.

GOING BALLISTIC With words like firing, smoking, barrel and going off, it's a natural progression to ballistic. 'It was going off. It was firing. The waves were smoking. Barrel after grinding barrel. Shit man, it was going fucking ballistic!'

GOING OFF When the surf is incredibly good, a surfer will say the surf is 'going off its face!' *Also* cooking, firing, pumping, smoking and going ballistic.

GOOF Swim. 'Let's go for a goof.' *See* gwaf.

GOOFED Stoned. 'Shew bru, I'm so goofed.'

GRAUNCH This onomatopoeic word is a perfect description of what it denotes. 'During the film, my boyfriend and I graunched in the back row' (During the movie we french kissed, rubbed, fondled, squeezed, gyrated and did everything short of penetration.)

GRAZE To eat. 'Let's go and graze' or 'What are you grazing?' or 'What's for graze mom?'

GRIP Get it off for the first time. 'John and I gripped each other last night.' *See* graunch.

GROMMET A young surfer of school-going age. Can be shortened to Grom. This almost affectionate, brotherly word rarely has negative connotations. However, when a grommet is pissing you off, or keeps dropping in on you, he automatically becomes a kook, or worse.

GUAVA Bottom, backside, bum or butt. 'His skateboard hit a rock and he fell on his guava.'

GUTSLIDER Bodyboarder. *See* doormat, sponge, speedbump.

GWAFFED Stoned. *See* gaffed. Gwaf means swim *See* goof.

GWARR, GWARRY, GWAT Female genitalia.

HALF-JACK A half-bottle of spirits.

HAK ('Huk') Pester, irritate.

HIT This is not used in the mafia sense in South Africa, much. Apart from its other meanings (to give someone a smack), it is widely used to denote a toke on a joint. 'Give me a hit of that joint please.'

HONE Stink. *See* hum. 'Your feet hone, bru'!

Hottie Someone who surfs really well. Also a descriptive term for a women, 'She's a hottie.'

Howzit The famous South African greeting. Short for 'How is it?' Try and refrain from saying, 'It's fine, thanks'. This will only lead to a funny look. A suitable reply is: 'No, fine,' which actually means 'Yes, I am fine.' The word 'no' is often taken to mean 'yes'. A real Afrikaner might reply to a 'Howzit', with this bewildering response: 'Ja, well, no fine.'

How's your mind? Are you mad?! This question, often in exasperation or irritation, refers to the mental stability of the subject, who has probably done something stupid, idiotic or irritating.

Hum Good surf, busy, smelly. There are three variations to this word. It's another way of describing good surf. But also, 'Surfers' Disco was humming last night.' (Really busy) and 'He hums like a skunk.' (He stinks.)

Impact Zone Also called the pit. It is where the waves break. At the Crayfish Factory on a 12' day, you don't really want to spend time there.

Isit? ('Izzit?') This conversational word is used widely and in response to just about anything. Derived perhaps from the English way of saying 'Is it really?' If you don't feel like participating in a conversation with a dik ou at a braai, but don't wish to appear rude, just say 'Isit' at appropiate gaps in his description of how he decapitated a Kudu with his bare hands.

Jacked, Jacking Rising swell, or organised person. 'The surf is jacking up' (The surf is getting bigger)' Or, 'That oke is jacked.' (That guy is really organised.)

Jags ('Yer–ag*s') Horny. 'Checking Pamela Anderson and Tommy Lee on the Internet made me so jags.'

Jammie Car. 'You have a kief jammie, bru.'

J–Bay Jeffrey's Bay, the mecca of surfing in South Africa.

Jeet To leave. See chuck, split, vaai.

Jislaaik Gee whizz.

Jissus An expression of amazement, similar to Jislaaik.

Jol ('Jawl') The word jol, like the word kief, is a generic South African word used not only by surfers. It refers to having a good time and can be used in any context. 'I am going on a jol (party).' 'I am having a jol (good time).' 'That spectacular wipeout at Super Tubes was a jol (rush).'

Just now Eventually or never. It depends. If someone says he will do something 'just now' it could be in 10 minutes or tomorrow. Or maybe he won't do it at all. 'I'll clean my room just now, Ma.'

Kaalgat ('Kaalg*at') Naked. When you are caught running around your girlfriend's house with no clothes on, you are kaalgat.

Kaffie, Kuif ('Kayph') Café. As you may gather, many South Africans don't care to pronounce words properly.

Kak ('Kuk') Shit. This is used in all sorts of weird and wonderful ways, in exactly the same way as the word 'shit'. Hence, 'Don't talk kak.' or 'Don't give me kak.'

Kap it ('Kup ut') To light a dagga pipe. Also 'Make it'.

The Kei ('Kye') The Transkei, former black homeland in the Eastern Cape.

Kief ('Kif') Almost as bland as 'nice' and equally wide-ranging. Can be used in any context. 'This chow is kief ek se.' 'I just had such a kief wave.'

King See legend.

Kittes ('Kittis') Clothes, gear. 'Jissus broer, you got lank marcha for the larney kittes.

Klap ('Klup') Slap. 'Ek sal jou a snotklap gee.' (I will give you a slap hard enough to make the snot fly.)

Klippies and Coke Brandy and Coke.

Kowie Port Alfred.

Knyp ('K–nape') Pinch, bite the bullet. When your bladder is full, and you can't go to the toilet, you 'knyp'.

Kook Someone who can't surf and gets in everyone's way. A kook is not necessarily a grommet, although a grommet can be a kook. Go figure.

KOPPE ('Korper') Heads. A 'kop' is a person's head. A 'koppie' is a small hill. But koppe refers to 'heads' of dope.

KREEF ('Kree–erf') Cape rock lobster. The waters of the Cape are home to millions of these crustaceans. Make friends with a local and go kreef diving, or bait them with a lobster pot (the kreef, not the locals). The daily bag limit (of kreef) is four, and the season is November to February.

KUS, KISH ('K'ss', 'keesh') Exhausted, tired. 'Jissus, my bru, that session at Supers made me totally kussed' or 'I am kished out.'

LANK A lot of something. 'There are lank people in the water.'

LARNEY Fancy or friend. A number of variations on this word: someone who is well-dressed ('Why are you dressed so larney?'), designer clothes ('Jees, you are wearing larney clothes.'), or a well-to-do function ('We went to a larney party that had caviar for pudding.') For coloured people in the Cape, it means 'Friend'. 'Hoesit my larnie!'

LEKKER An Afrikaans word meaning nice, this word is used by all language groups to express approval. 'Lekker jol.' (Nice party)

LEGEND Hero, good guy. In the Eastern Cape, when the party is ripping, and everyone starts getting all soppy and sentimental, they might start calling each other 'legends'. Also heard when someone pulls off a lank clever move. 'Jono, you LEGEND!' Can be shortened to 'lej'. 'That session was lej, bru!'

LIGHTEY Youngster. 'That lightey is a pretty good surfer, for a grommet.'

LOMP Lethargic.

LUSIKISIKI LIME GREENS A variety of dope.

MADIBA The clan name for former President Mandela, but universally used as an affectionate nickname. His full name is Nelson Rolihlahla ('Roli–shla–shla') Mandela.

MAJAT Low grade dope.

MAL Mad. 'That ou is mal'.

MALAWI COBS A marijuana variety.

MARCHA Money. 'Jissus bru, you got lank marcha for the larney kittes ek se.'

MARMITE Australians have Vegemite, we have Marmite. Like its poor Australian cousin, Marmite is a salty vegetable extract resembling crude oil.

MIX Tobacco to dilute strong dope.

MOER ('Moor–r') Hit, punch. Another Afrikaans word meaning to hit someone. 'I will moer you if you take off on my wave.'

MOFFIE ('Moffee') A derogeratory term for a gay person. But also used in jest by gays.

MOZZIE Mosquito.

MULL To prepare the dope.

MULLET It does not necessarily refer to the fish of this name used as bait, but someone who is crazy, or whacky. 'That ou is a mullet.' He doesn't have to be insane, (one beer short of a sixpack), just eccentric or strange.

MUNGED To be stoned or goofed.

MUNGBERRY Someone who smokes too much dope.

MUNGER A really ugly person who does sif things.

NECK Bottleneck pipe

NOOIT ('Noy–t') No way. Another way of saying no, but also a sign of incredulous response. If you have just heard that a South African beat Kelly Slater to win the world surfing champs, you would say, 'Nooit! Are you serious?'

NOUGHT ('Nawt') No. Used like nooit. Used in the Eastern Cape as a reference to a person's asshole. 'I fell on my nought.'

NUMBER Joint. See also doob, spleef, neck, bane, slowboat.

OKE ('Oak') Guy, chap, bloke. You can also say 'ou', pronounced 'Oh.'

ON A MISSION When you're determined to complete a task, you are 'on a mission'.

OVER THE FALLS The classic surf wipeout, when the lip of the wave sucks you over and you take a trip into the air, followed by a double impact (wave and water) and several cycles in a salty washing machine.

PAP ('Pup') Boiled corn meal. The staple diet of many South Africans. Eaten mostly in the townships, it is often found at braais. It has the appearance of wet plaster, but is delicious. Pap is versatile. It's eaten as sweet porridge, or as part of a main course.

PARK OFF Chill out, relax. 'Shall we park off and watch the *Rip Curl Search* video for the 40th time?' It can also mean to sit down, as in, 'Why don't you park here?'

PARK A TIGER To vomit or puke. Sometimes referred to as the multi-coloured yawn.

PAVEMENT Sidewalk (US).

PE Port Elizabeth.

PEKKIE, PIKKIE Derived from 'picannin', it means 'small child'. Eastern Cape whites often call black people pekkies. Not a nice word when used in this context, due to racist connotations.

PIPE The orifice through which dagga (dope) is smoked. 'Kap a pipe my broer.'

PIT This is where you don't want to be when a huge set wave is breaking. It refers to the impact zone, the area where the waves break.

PITCHIE A quaint term for a dagga seed.

PLUCK Mindset. You may say to someone who has just delivered obscure reasoning for doing something, 'How's your pluck?' (Where are you coming from?) The variation to this is, 'How's your mind?' Pluck refers to a distracted, even deranged, state of mind. 'He was on a pluck when he dived off the roof.' (He was on some kind of weird trip when he dived off the roof.)

POES Cunt, nasty person. This word has a number of different meanings. It is a swear word, mostly used to berate someone. 'You stupid poes'. Also used to describe a thoroughly nasty, unlikeable person; someone who has 'pulled an action', or ripped someone off perhaps. 'That ou is a poes'.

POEPHOL ('Poo–pawl') Idiot, twit.

POMP ('Pormp') Bonk, have sex. The crude, but popular, description of the carnal act.

PONDOLOAND FEVER Not a tropical disease,

just a general lethargy brought on by the mindboggling quality of the dope.

PORSIE ('Paw–z–y') House, spot, place, 'Should we watch videos at your porsie?'

PULL AN ACTION Someone who has done something very undesirable, such as driving over a friend's surfboard.

PULL IN To enter the barrel or the tube is to 'pull in'. It is also used as an invitation. 'Pull in to our jol tonight broer' (Come to our party tonight, brah.) Also used to describe a kiss, 'They pulled in to each other.'

PUMPING Good surf. *See* also, cooking, firing, going off, going ballistic, smoking.

RAGE To have a rage is to go on a serious party, to push the limits of social etiquette and subject the body to a variety of excessive stimulants and stimuli.

RAT Not to be confused with the furry creature with buck teeth, although youngsters who surf, many of them beginners, are viewed in the same way, if not worse. At least real rats don't drop in on you.

RAVE The rave is similar to a Rage, but tends to be a little less intense. Having a rave suggests more of a good time. In other words, being able to remember what you did the night before. 'I had such a rave with that girl I met on the beach.'

RIP What a good surfer does when riding a wave. 'He rips it apart.' Also refers to rip currents in the sea.

ROBOT Traffic light. Peculiar term for a traffic light. But then, we only got TV in the mid 1970s.

ROCK UP To arrive. Old fashioned way of saying 'pull in'. You don't tell anyone you're on the way, you just rock up.

ROOIBOS Red bush tea. A tannin-free herb tea made from the *Aspalathus linearis* bush.

RUSH A spurt of adrenalin. 'I got such a rush riding that 15' barrel.'

SAFE The classic South African reference to 'being cool'. Pretty much outdated.

SALAD Bits of marijuana sucked through the gerrick into one's mouth.

SAMP An African food made from rough corn. It is starchy and is often eaten with haricot or red beans, dunked in gravy stew. Delicious.

SARMIE Sandwich. Kids sometimes take a sarmie to school in the morning.

SCALE To scale something is to steal it. A person who is 'scaly' is a scumbag or sleazy type. See also skate.

SCHNARF Cocaine.

SCORE When you go and buy something, usually drugs. Also refers to gratification when the goal is reached after looking for sex.

SECTION Part of a wave. When you hit a section called Impossibles at Jay Bay, you get pitted in an awesome barrel from which you will be lucky to emerge. When you hit the gooey rooibaard section of a six-blade slowboat in the Kei, you will be lucky to emerge with wits and IQ intact.

SHARK BISCUITS Bodyboarders (Aus).

SHIFT Fast. 'That car was really shifting.'

SHOT Thanks. 'Shot my broer.'

SHREDDING This pertains, once again, to those awesome carving, ripping, tearing moves being pulled off by, say, Kelly Slater.

SIF ('Suf') Disgusting. *See* mif. A shortened version of syphillus, sif doesn't necessarily refer to disease, but could refer to a gangrenous coral wound, an overused long drop toilet, a car accident or a chorb.

SIS ('Sus') Yuck. 'Sis, man, you just kotched (vomited) on my wetsuit.'

SJOE ('Shoe') Expletive. 'Sjoe bru, that wave was awesome.' *Also* shew and shwee.

SKATE Unsavoury character.

SKAY Watch out. *See* chips. If a car is heading for you, and you haven't noticed, your friend will shout 'Skay!'

SKEEF ('Skee–urf') Crooked (provocative). 'Are you checking me skeef, China?' This often precedes a brawl or barnie.

SKEEM Think, opinion. 'You skeem?' (You think so?) 'What do you skeem?' (What do you think?)

SKELM ('Skellum') A crook or thief. A streetwise operator who deals in petty crime.

SKINNER Gossip.

SKITSELS The debris, or detritus, left at the bottom of the jar, or bank packet, after you used up the best of your stash.

SKOLLY ('Skaw–llie') Sleazy ruffian. Also referred to as a 'skommie' or a 'skate'.

SKOP Kick. Can also be used as in 'My girlfriend skopped me out for surfing too much.'

SKRIK ('Skruk') A fright. After being held down for 30 seconds in the kelp at Crayfish Factory, you might get a bit of a 'skrik'.

SKYF ('Skayf') Spliff, to smoke. 'Let's make a skyf' refers to the first, naturally.

SLAP CHIPS ('Slup chups') When French Fries are thick and long and don't go crispy in the oil. They are soft and stodgy, ideal for mixing in mounds of tomato sauce or vinegar, or both.

SLASH Piss, leak. 'I'm taking a slash.'

SLIP SLOPS Mostly called 'slops', they are what Australians call thongs or sandals. The proper slops are made from rubber and have a strap between your big toe and its partner.

SLOT IN Another way of pulling into a tube. 'Peter was perfectly slotted.' (Peter rode the tube perfectly.)

SLUK To steal or to have a drink. You can sluk a TV (steal) or have a sluk of someone's drink (sip).

SLUMTOWN, SLUMMIES Affectionate nickname for East London.

SMOKING Good surf. *Also* cooking, firing, going off, going ballistic, smoking.

SNOEK This is a fierce fish found in the sea off Cape Town. It has sharp teeth and is long and narrow like a barracuda. It tastes great when fresh. Dried, salted snoek can be eaten as is, or served in a stew called 'smoorvis'.

SNOEP This is not a fish, but a noun or verb referring to extreme stinginess.

SORRY Excuse me. While used for its global

meaning, as an apology, South Africans have managed to mutate it further. 'Sorry, can I just get past.'

SOUTHEASTER Strong trade wind that comes from the southeast and flattens Cape Town for large portions of the summer. *See* Cape Doctor.

SOSATIE Kebab. Made from either chicken, lamb or beef, this is often interspersed with pieces of tomato, green pepper, onion and sometimes fruit, especially apricot.

SPAT OUT The fortunate few who have been spat out of a tube with a burst of spray when compressed air caught in the swirling cylinder is suddenly released.

SPEEDBUMP, SPONGE Bodyboarder. *See* doormat, gutslider, shark biscuit.

SPLEEF Splif (South African variation).

SPOOK AND DIESEL Cane spirits and coke.

SQUIF ('Skwif') Skew, crooked.

SQUEEZE Girlfriend.

STAUNCH Dik, big, strong.

STOKED Totally amped up, revved up.

STOP, STOPPE ('Stawp') A 'section' of dope. If you buy a stop you are scoring weed in a specific package, usually a sausage-shaped parcel wrapped in newspaper.

STROPPY Cheeky.

STUKKEND ('Stuk–int') To the max, filled up, full. There are a number of variations, such as 'I'm going to moer you stukkend if you do that again' or 'When she left me my heart was stukkend' or 'I was stukkend last night' (very drunk).

STUKKIE Sexist term for a woman, or man. From the Afrikaans word stuk, which means 'piece'. A stukkie is a 'little piece'.

STYLING When you're styling, everything clicks into place and you find yourself surfing like Kelly Slater, Tom Curren and 'insert–favourite–surfer–here' rolled into one.

SUKKEL ('Sukul') Struggle.

SURFARI Surf trip.

SUSS Savvy. 'Having a bit of suss', is to be sharp, knowledgeable or street–wise. 'I have

sussed it out' (I have worked it out).

SWAZI REDS A potent cannabis vintage.

TAKKIES Sneakers, trainers, running shoes.

TEARING A hot surfer in the process of ripping up the waves. Also rip, carve, cook, shred and style.

THE MOER IN (roll the r) Very angry.

TRANSKEI GOLD A cannabis vintage from Transkei.

TUNE ('Choon') To tell, to talk, to provoke. For instance, 'Don't tune me grief' (Don't give me your bullshit) or 'Are you tuning me kak?' (Are you giving me shit?). 'Tune me the ages' (Tell me the time).

VROT ('Frort') Rotten, putrid. Used by all language groups to describe something highly undesirable, or smelly, or rotten. It can also mean drunk to the point of being completely paralytic. 'I was vrot last night'

WASTED Paralytic drunk or totally high. 'I was completely wasted at the party.'

WEDGE When there is a break near a wall, pier or jetty. The waves come in, rebound off the wall and travel sideways into the on-coming swell. This pushes up the wave in the middle, forming an A-frame wedge.

WHACKED *See* wasted.

WHACKY BACKY Dope.

WHAT KIND? Don't be a jerk. If your friend has just spewed out the side of your car, you would call indignantly 'What kind?'

WOBBLY Panic attack, fit of rage. 'Peter threw a wobbly after someone drove over his new 7'8" custom surfboard.'

WUSS, WUSSIE Wimp, pansie, weakling.

YURRUH Variation of Jissus.

WETTIE A drink, refreshment. 'Hey brah, I'm lank thirsty, lets grab a wettie.'

WINDMILL Name for a waveski rider. *See* Goatboat.

WHEAT Dope.

ZOL ('Zawl') A joint commonly rolled out of a piece of newspaper and stuck together with saliva.

ZONKED Completely stoned.

INDEX

Surf Spots